Psychotherapy and the Abrasive Patient

Psychotherapy and the Abrasive Patient

E. Mark Stern, Editor

Iona College, New Rochelle, New York

The Haworth Press
New York

Psychotherapy and the Abrasive Patient has also been published as *The Psychotherapy Patient*, Volume 1, Number 1, Fall 1984.

The Haworth Press, Inc., 28 East 22 Street, New York, NY 10010

Library of Congress Cataloging in Publication Data
Main entry under title:

Psychotherapy and the abrasive patient

Also published as: The Psychotherapy patient, vol. 1, no. 1.
Bibliography: p.
1. Abrasiveness (Psychology)—Addresses, essays, lectures. 2. Psychotherapy—Addresses, essays, lectures. I. Stern, E. Mark, 1929-   . [DNLM: 1. Physician-patient relations. 2. Psychotherapy—Methods. 3. Personality disorders—Therapy. W1 PS87 v.1. no.1 / WM 420 P9753]
RC569.5.A24P79   1984   616.85'8   84-6644
ISBN 0-86656-325-3

Psychotherapy and the Abrasive Patient

The Psychotherapy Patient
Volume 1, Number 1

CONTENTS

Psychotherapy
and the
Abrasive Patient

Welcome to the Reader

Allow me to extend a hearty greeting to you on behalf of the Editorial Board and the publisher of *The Psychotherapy Patient*. Still in its bib-and-jumper stage, this newest addition to the family of the journals published by The Haworth Press represents a unique attempt at gathering clinical findings and experiential commentaries on attribute-focused clinical practice. Although not intended to replace established psychiatric, psychological, and casework nosology, this journal's quest to better understand commonly ascribed attributes of patients in psychotherapy represents an important step in linking the therapeutic hunch with appropriate clinical practice. This focus on attributes is meant to portray the ways and means patients define themselves within the social orbit.

We begin our series with an exploration of the *abrasive patient*. In so doing we welcome each of you to better read the signals of the abrasive since most such patients have an ominous capacity to rub others in a nettlesome way. Yet while the abrasive galvanizes irritation, s/he may be attempting to awaken the fonts of personal strength and social capability.

Some abrasive individuals are only so within a clinical setting, others with their families or intimates, and more than a few in public settings such as crowds and traffic jams.

Abrasiveness is a way of meeting the world. As an attribute it is a means of defending, creating, and often destroying self-possession. On close inspection, many attributes transcend caste and class. Yet there are times when abrasiveness or any attribute serves as a source of misinformation. It is then that the attribute may throw dust in the eyes of the casual observer. This journal's purpose is to clarify the several vital messages attributes actually render.

By now it should be clear that the attribute is accessorial to the continuing formation of personality. As a qualitative assist, the attribute serves to express essential aspects of the individual life-style without necessarily being its final epitaph.

In another vein, while an attribute may be thought to be a surfacing of a particular set of psychodynamics, it more appropriately belongs to interpersonal predilections and propensities. Regardless of such psychodynamics of underlying social and familial systems, the attribute remains an expression of individuality. Thus psychotherapists are wise to acknowledge the attribute as a calling card rather than a total expression of personhood.

This journal of attribute-based practice will in each issue strive to explore what makes for expressive distinctiveness in psychotherapy patients. In this spirit, it will draw freely from the many cisterns of theory, research, and clinical experience. Since it will not proffer fixed formats, this journal's unevenness in tone should be regarded as its unique contact with divergent clinical views. It is this Editor's hope that *The Psychotherapy Patient* will become a worthy and informative companion to those who wish to keep faith with the growing edge of clinical practice.

E. Mark Stern, Ed.D.
Editor

The Move Toward Responsibility
Psychotherapy and the Abrasive Patient

E. Mark Stern

> ". . . anger and then love."
> Izette de Forest

The thought of bringing this first issue of *The Psychotherapy Patient* to life on the theme of The Abrasive Patient required my thinking back over what one particular patient had taught me. I write about Carlo as my substantial introduction to the ways and means of encountering abrasiveness in the practice of psychotherapy.

Carlo is a real person. But, for this exercise, the surrounding facts of his origins and life have been substantially camouflaged. Carlo personally helped me shape what I write about him. He did this as a way of helping me introduce some seminal constructs in the management of other abrasive patients. As my words will reveal, Carlo's intemperate levelings with me, his therapist, were the stepping stones to his own attainments and ultimate fulfillments as a responsible citizen, parent, and spouse.

* * *

Carlo was used to flaunting his aristocratic background. He claimed that he felt like an emotionally paralyzed exile. Carlo was an 11-year-old when he and his newly divorced mother left their native land. Carlo's father chose to break all ties with his ex-wife and son. And to complicate matters, Carlo's mother established herself in a lesbian relationship soon after arriving in the United States.

Despite the abandonment, Carlo's father did ultimately leave him the bulk of his estate. He died some 6 months into Carlo's therapy. Carlo was then in his early 30s. Despite his success as a landscape architect, Carlo

---

E. Mark Stern, Ed.D., completed his clinical studies at Columbia University (1955) and at the Institute of the National Psychological Association for Psychoanalysis. Besides his private practice in psychotherapy and psychoanalysis, Dr. Stern is Professor in the Graduate Division of Pastoral Counseling, Iona College, New Rochelle, New York, and on the faculty of the American Institute for Psychotherapy and Psychoanalysis in New York City. Dr. Stern is a Diplomate in Clinical Psychology of the American Board of Professional Psychology.

continued to act on the assumption that people were purposely avoiding him. The resulting haughty manner abraded most everyone. Through the earlier months of his therapy Carlo complained of compelling dreads. He began to make a habit of washing his hands before and after every consultation. He expressed marked fury whenever the waiting-room lavatory was in use. Three patients were on several occasions surprised to hear Carlo angrily rapping on the door of the occupied facilities. He never directly mentioned these incidents. Carlo did, however, let me know how fearful he was of his mother's wrath when, as a young child, he locked the bathroom door. It was apparent that a locked bathroom door indicated the possibility of the child masturbating. Noting the correlation between his mother's accusations and Carlo's latter-day abrasiveness played a significant role in his therapy.

For the time being, Carlo's veiled voyeurism expressed itself in his vaunting his professional and artistic accomplishments, though this vaunting was set against Carlo's incessant scoffing at his professional colleagues.

Throughout the course of his therapy Carlo regularly blew up at the alleged dishonesty of his closest advisers, including his attorneys and accounting firm. Proudly Carlo boasted of having made his advisers "back down" in their fees, the amount of services rendered, and in their pride. Throughout our work, Carlo maintained an accurate count of the allotted consultation time. At one point he insisted on an extra session to make up for the minutes I spent on the phone. Carlo felt it his right to keep his auto headlights on high beam regardless of the discomfort it caused drivers of oncoming cars, as well as those directly in front of him. He registered surprise and no little arrogant pride when he was given two traffic summons for his refusal to dim the lights when signaled to do so by a traffic officer.

Carlo's wife did not trust him. She retained her own attorney specifically for her dealings with him. Indeed the marriage appeared to be based on the model of a financial business arrangement. Carlo mentioned that he'd given a large sum of money to Paula as part of their premarital agreement. Each kept separate accountings. Paula regularly demanded increased sums of money for her various spending sprees. At one point Carlo informed me that Paula refused to conceive a child until he put in her name a considerable portion of his family's fortune and his deceased mother's jewels. Nevertheless, the marriage appeared to maintain itself and even appeared to be emotionally viable. All this despite the fact that Carlo regularly contemplated hiring a private surveillance service to watch over his wife's day-to-day life. Forever looking for Paula's fatal flaws, Carlo appeared to be genuinely disappointed when there was no evidence that she acted in any way but faithful to the marriage.

Soon after I began to work with Carlo, Paula entered psychoanalysis with a classical analyst. Not long into her treatment, Carlo claimed that he too felt the need for as many sessions with me as Paula had with her doctor. At first I questioned this "even-Steven" attitude but later agreed to his plan in hopes that he would begin to see that there might be something to lose in his having to "keep even" with Paula. Soon, however, it appeared that our frequent sessions were, in fact, Carlo's *only* significant social contact outside of the marriage. In all other social activities Carlo felt like an outsider. This feeling continued despite the fact that he and Paula were, as individuals and as a couple, frequently sought out by several "worthwhile" people.

Carlo regularly acted like an angry youngster. In the few social situations he engaged in, he was eventually seen as a despoiler. He spent hours during sessions literally sneering at my neighborhood, my tastes, his notion of my family background, and his stereotypes of the whole psychiatric-psychological professional world. When he felt he'd gone too far, he'd try to redeem himself by allowing that I might be a notch or two above "those others." This attempt at conciliation was understandable in the face of the fact that Carlo had been twice abandoned, first by his father and then by his mother. His mother was alive during the early work we did together. Through several recent years his mother's extreme stance as a radical feminist/lesbian seemed to include the conviction that most males were negative forces in Western society. Her death revived earlier feelings of abandonment as a result of her association with man-hating groups.

Carlo maintained an almost studied, stodgy manner. Yet it became obvious that Carlo's snobbery was his way of *appearing* grown-up. In the absence of *feeling* grown-up, Carlo lived on the brink of his destructive impulses. Malicious and loutish, he confirmed his existence through his irritation. There were those occasions when Carlo would place his hot coffee container on a fragile waiting-room end table. Seeing that he'd damaged some of the veneer, Carlo fumed about my stinginess in not providing a more suitable stand or platform for such objects. It was of course pretty hard not to note the dozen or more dated magazines that might have served as improvised coasters. On the one occasion on which I mentioned the "coaster" idea, Carlo angrily claimed that my waiting room needed radical improvement.

Because of an inherited fortune, Carlo was in a position to buy a considerable amount of common stock in an expanding chemical company. Using his stock as a lever, Carlo made a game of popping in to the company's major distributing center—ostensibly to keep a self-appointed stockholder's "quality control" on the working operation of the organization. He was able to admit that he received perverse enjoyment in making the middle management "quake." He claimed that he had created a "necessary climate of fear" by threatening to "dump" his shares. Indeed he did

fulfill these threats, even at a financial loss, because of management's refusal to nominate him for the corporation's Board of Directors. Later it
became clear that he would gladly go down any precipice with open eyes
in the face of social rejection.

Carlo boasted of the perverse satisfaction he experienced in withholding gratuities from rude waiters and taxicab drivers. Mild provocation
worked to serve as opportunities for the worse of his vengeful actions.
Carlo mentioned an incident in which his body blocked an entry gate at
the airport. He had been reading the last of an article in his newspaper.
The impatient urgings of the agent at the gate finally got Carlo to move on
board. But he said that he'd "had it" with having to wait endlessly while
the plane waited its turn to take off, and he wrote a letter to the airline's
president complaining of the "insolent" behavior of the agent.

It took time to learn that Carlo's abrasiveness was his means of gaining
some advantage over the failure he experienced in personal relationships.
Although he felt some marginal satisfaction in occasional attempts at socialization, his obsession with gaining an advantage over others was his
indication of how broken he felt. His overtures at gaining some personal
credibility were masked by his dismaying behavior.

I attempted to thread my way into Carlo's self-system by being supportive of his attempts to gain personal respect. Even though I quaked at his
constant complaints about my neighborhood and working space, I tended
to respond to these critical laments by asking for his ideas for alternatives.
This took several odd turns. There was the time when Carlo actually took
it upon himself to visit a real-estate agent in order to secure listings of
houses in an upgraded neighborhood he felt would suit me. I took the opportunity to thank him for his efforts and praise him for his thoughtful-
ness. My response evoked a muted surprise in him. Carlo had apparently
expected me to boil with indignation rather than smile upon his efforts.

Carlo's attacks were rarely veiled. One day he mentioned my neigh-
bor's unrepaired sidewalk. He used this as an opportunity to further berate me, saying that if I insisted on living in such miserable surroundings
I was probably making a statement about what I thought of my patients.
When I asked Carlo why he insisted on seeing me rather than someone in
a more "acceptable" neighborhood, his answer was abrupt: Since he had
begun this "strange exercise" with me, he suggested that he could not see
himself going through it all over again with another "grandstander."

Halfway into his psychotherapy and following a prolonged overseas
trip, Carlo went through a near major breakdown. At the time I found it
difficult to put the pieces together, except for one new torment. Carlo
once again suspected that his wife was having an affair. He couldn't be
more specific, but used his agony to inform me that he had a great urge to
deal me a set of swift kicks in my groin. He said he had difficulty containing a wish to seek out his wife's analyst in order to perform fellatio on

him. Carlo then asked my help in assisting him in becoming better contained. When I suggested that he feared his wife was in love with her analyst, Carlo's only thought was to seduce the man homosexually. In the meantime Paula had been making obvious strides in her analysis. I noted that her increasing self-esteem made Carlo restless and fearful of losing her. When I mentioned her emerging confidence, Carlo sat up straight and glowered at me. I decided not to back off and I asked him to take a chance in examining the hatred he felt for his mother's "strength." This was followed by my recommending that Paula's wish to be strong was not an abdication from the marriage but her attempt at reaching out to a better sense of their bond. Carlo's fear prevailed even as he himself began to wrestle with the possibility of joining his mother in her nightmarish campaign against all intimacies. The exacerbation of this scourge had gone to extremes—taking the form of an angry homosexual panic. His stated wish to suck and bite "the enemy" heralded the primitive urges originally meant to contain the enemy but which ultimately worked as psychic equivalents of total capitulation. If Paula were to leave him, he would win over her analyst. Still he felt that he would fail in this attempt to reach his "father" in the person of his wife's doctor. This sexualized fantasy terrified him and he responded to it with a felt need to punish me for not saving his mother, that is, Paula, for him.

Like any agitated soul, Carlo was in need of immediate relief. Yet the danger of abetting his feelings of helplessness and impotence had to be avoided. I retained a steady focus on his attempts at self-assertion, never minimizing the destructive fall-out which had resulted from the "kicking" and "biting." I continued to stress his personal power, moving in the direction of helping him reestablish an effective base as a strong loving son. Ultimately his unfounded suspicions about his wife having an extramarital affair seemed to diminish. As a result, Carlo began to rebuild the rudiments of a social decorum. We both agreed that a significant portion of his abrasiveness helped assure him of a latent but emerging effectiveness. As Carlo's behavior changed he made it clear that he knew I had been on his side. I had become the father he'd never known and he loved me for it. He appeared to be increasingly cognizant that I would not knowingly abandon him and that he could count on me during periods of tribulation. Through it all, Carlo's uncertainties were never far from his new-found faith. For one, he worried about my physical well-being. He felt bolstered by my increasing promises to be with him as he launched himself into maturity. He made excellent use of the frequent contacts with me as his chosen way of providing himself with the sustained care he felt he absolutely needed.

Carlo's abrasiveness did not vanish like the mist. When he occasionally found himself caught in the shoals of frustration, Carlo felt the upsurge of small rages. For example, the year Carlo became a biological father in his own right, he found himself involuntarily seething with the brand new challenges. This time, however, his irritation appeared to result from the obligations of parenthood. In such instances Carlo's abrasiveness was his primitive means of establishing gradients of personal power and competence.

Like Carlo, abrasive patients commonly require their therapists to stay in touch with their needs to achieve social responsibility. Experience teaches that no effective therapy is realized unless the abrasive modes are seen as central to the quest for personal credibility. Carlo's predicament made clear how this quest had gone wild. Throughout the course of his treatment, I as therapist first became an object of derision before being seen as a worthy fellow traveler. Derision as an accompaniment of abrasiveness is likely to be linked with early figures in patients' lives. Throughout my work with Carlo the transferential abrasiveness demonstrated how he needed to maintain an obsessive ambivalence around his obdurate parents. Through his continued resentment, these primary figures remained contained and intact. Incorporation of these seminal figures was "the precursor of later . . . destructive attitudes" (Fenichel, 1945, p. 38) and was in a sense his means of destroying them. My continuing presence in Carlo's life made it possible to give meaning to the ambivalence of needing and not needing a responsible parent. The transfer of training from the positive doctor/patient encounter to a broader meeting with significant others in his contemporary world allowed for some resolution of this ambivalence.

This approach is in substantial agreement with the cognitive reality therapy of Glasser (1965) and the experiential analytic work of de Forest (1954). In tune with Glasser, my work with Carlo found me encouraging him to ponder his emerging sense of social responsibility. My positive regard for what he was doing with his life thus became a value in itself. Furthermore, my respect for his struggle helped to highlight the fact that even his abrasiveness had a place in his struggle for personal values. Even so, the weight of Carlo's abrasive bearing eventually had to be reckoned with as a counterproductive addiction. Similar to the position fostered by Alcoholics Anonymous, Carlo's destructive abrasiveness had to be owned up to fully before he had the slightest possibility of getting a handle on it and steering it to productive ends.

My work with Carlo seemed to go through three major phases. The first witnessed the de-structuring of behavior which, while abrasive to others, appeared to provide Carlo with a temporary sense of safe passage in social relationships. This de-structuring was accompanied by a sense of seeing his walls topple about him. It was up to me as his therapist to *be there* throughout this loss of a "safe base" in order for my presence to be available for Carlo's having to deal with a surfacing sense of helplessness and regret. When a resulting tenderness began to interfere with his daily transactions, Carlo needed to test the limits of my care and concern for him.

During the second phase of treatment, Carlo needed to reconcile his abrasiveness with the wish to become more responsive to social demands. Once this period was reached, what remained of his abrasive behavior had to be viewed as a level of understandable impatience in his quest for love and acceptance. Here the outflow of newer capacities developed in tandem with some increase in anxiety. This anxiety motivated Carlo to approach the next steps of his journey with caution, leaving him little choice but to return to some measure of his former abrasiveness. As time moved on, Carlo made several obvious attempts at reaching a cohesive social maturity which, while at times having some resemblance to abrasiveness, provided him with new options in being with others.

The third and final phase of his treatment chronicled Carlo's sensitized awareness of the role of the differences between destructive and constructive anger. Here the groundwork for the conflicting and alternating expressions of abrasiveness and tenderness became an established part of his emotional repertoire. It now became Carlo's task to become confirmed "by the very strength of the emotional conflict itself" (de Forest, 1954, p. 94). The value of shifting antagonisms and affections allowed him to make a fuller use of his new-found selfhood—one in which he became a responsive/responsible adult. This last phase of therapy took several years. Throughout all these phases, it remained my task to maintain a merited respect and reverence for the courageous efforts and endurance Carlo perfected in his personal awakenings. Happily, Carlo was able to construct an effective power base through which a new relationship to his world vis-à-vis his therapy was established.

* * *

For Carlo as for other abrasive patients, psychotherapy comes closest to being a vital necessity in the process of socialization. Correspondingly, it is the abrasive patient who, by necessity, provides the therapist with an ever-present challenge to maintain a consistently high level of professional skill and responsibility. The journey from abrasiveness to sound social resonance requires an extended awareness of the individual's personal capacities. Those in psychotherapy are expected to learn to embrace better forms of communication in their respective quests for a response to the communal milieu. But in order to take the necessary steps the patient must be willing to see in his or her abrasiveness the elements of care and concern. He or she can best achieve these ends by a willingness to see that abrasiveness is the natural expression of estrangement. Only then can the patient move from an angry abrasiveness to the possibility of a responsive love.

REFERENCES

de Forest, I. (1954). *The leaven of love*. New York: Harper.
Fenichel, O. (1945). *The psychoanalytic theory of neurosis*. New York: W.W. Norton.
Glasser, W. (1965). *Reality therapy*. New York: Harper & Row.

Abrasiveness:
Descriptive and Dynamic Issues

Barry J. Wepman
Molly W. Donovan

INTRODUCTION

We conceived this paper as a study of abrasiveness and of the abrasive patient in general. However, because a high percentage of our patients are women, we began to concentrate on abrasive women patients and a pattern of similarities among these women began to emerge. The few abrasive male patients whom we were able to discuss seemed not to fit the pattern entirely (e.g., some historical variables), so a separate study of them would seem to be appropriate. This paper, then, is our conceptualization of abrasiveness as a human character pattern, its functions and effects, and of the dynamics of the abrasive women patients we've observed.

ABRASION AS A METAPHOR

The abrasive person affects a unique presence, whether in psychotherapy or in the world at large. This person attempts to make an impression on others, but does so in a way that is often experienced by the others as intrusive, assaultive, or annoying. Like grit in a motor, an abrasive individual grates on the surface of the other, wearing the other down.

This is not to say that either abrasion or abrasiveness exists only as a negative characteristic. No two objects found in nature can oppose each other in an interactive way without friction and the loss to the other of at least a few atoms of substance. Some abrasion is destructive, causing parts to wear out and need replacement, yet other abrasion is useful, as in

Barry J. Wepman, Ph.D., received his doctorate in clinical psychology from the University of Houston. He is Clinical Assistant Professor in the Department of Psychiatry and Mental Sciences at the University of Medicine and Dentistry of New Jersey-New Jersey Medical School. Dr. Wepman also maintains a private practice in Florham Park.

Molly W. Donovan, Ph.D., received her doctorate in clinical psychology from George Washington University in 1976. She is in private practice and is Co-Director of the Washington Women's Psychotherapy Center in Washington, D.C.

cleansing powder or sandpaper, gently removing accretions and keeping surfaces freshened. Often in the manufacture of precision dynamic systems, the final step is to allow meshing parts to "grind in" against one another in order to achieve the best functioning with the closest mechanical tolerances. Similarly, a certain period of friction often occurs in relationships between two people who come very close.

We have found the entire metaphor of abrasion to be illuminating when applied to human processes: In every interaction between two people there is wear; people make impressions upon one another that may be deep and lasting or may be superficial and transitory, worn away by succeeding contact with others. There are some people who are soft and malleable and make little impression, and others who are adamantine. How abrasive one person is, how easily worn down is another, may be seen as determined by several metaphorical variables: As people are hard, closed, and rough edged, their abrasiveness increases. The extent to which others are worn down may depend on their hardness and on the duration of contact and its intensity. Where one can withdraw s/he can reduce the wear s/he experiences, and, clearly more solid people are less vulnerable than are softer ones who are unable to escape or close themselves to the damaging contact.

THE ABRASIVE PERSON

Notable are several aspects of the abrasive personality: the ability of the abrasive person to hold onto others while rubbing them raw with his/her behavior; the push-pull of desire for contact versus the fear of being damaged that leads to the alienating behavior; the need for being heard and accepted coupled with the difficulty in hearing and accepting another; the tendency of the abrasive person to "keep on coming" in the absence of receptivity. These observations led us to conclude that the abrasive position is one of ambivalence: There is a need for nurturance and a fear of opening the self to receive it. From this grows our belief that the abrasive person coming to therapy is starving, even if surrounded by a banquet. This, in fact, has often been our experience. The abrasive person is frustrating and frustrated, irritating and irritated, often has a strong negative impact on those around them, and is emotionally isolated.

The people we have perceived as abrasive tend to have a high need for human contact, but a fear of emotional openness and intimacy. Their behavior is abrasive not only in that it is wearing on others but also because it is relentless. They keep coming on without regard to the signals that others send them, and they tend to be insensitive to others' needs in a way that is painful and may, in some circumstances, be profoundly damaging. Where a hard, abrasive person is in prolonged contact with one who is much softer, significant and lasting damage can be done.

A.D. was a woman in her late 20s, the daughter of an abrasive mother. She rarely made eye contact and spent many of the therapy sessions speaking very little; for a long time she hardly seemed present at all. After years, she began to talk more freely, but even then there was little contact as she spoke mostly in tight monologic narratives. Her responses to therapeutic interventions were unpredictable: Some interventions seemed to have little impact, and, at other times, a very mild statement could foster a retreat which might last for several sessions. The overall impression she created suggested that she had sustained early damage to her personality structure. She seemed to have been deeply abraded. Her mother had been described by various family members as loud, insensitive, and full of energy. It was clear that A.D. was both strongly drawn to her mother and negatively affected by her. Once A.D. described an interaction between her mother and an infant nephew: Her mother, she said, seemed to have no awareness of the baby's having moods or giving signals about his receptivity to approach. Rather, if she felt like playing with the baby, she would play with him, whether the baby was reacting positively or was stiff and avoidant.

A picture began to emerge of this overbearing, narcissistic, woman interacting with her emotionally sensitive daughter oblivious to her daughter's reactions. Over time she wore through A.D.'s defenses and began to abrade her fundamental character structure.

The characteristics mentioned here—hardness, insensitivity to external cues, and intrusiveness—begin the exploration of the abrasive personality. The tendency to disregard others and, in an autistic way, to steamroll ahead to keep contact, whether it is reciprocated or not, seems to be a cardinal characteristic. The abrasive person makes little differentiation about the quality of attention or response received. She or he does not take cues from the other in order to enable better communication; communication is not the aim. Attention to the abrasive person appears to be the goal of the behavior.

S.C. is a prototype of the abrasive person. In conversation, she will undercut others present, minimizing or criticizing them, bringing the focus to herself, outdoing the speaker with a story of her own. If anyone objects or tries to return to the original story she typically interjects herself again until people either leave or withdraw into silence. She then keeps trying to reengage those around her. They must either ignore her, comply with her demands, or confront her, none of which is effective because of the denseness of the armoring below the surface of her roughness; to attempt direct confrontation inevitably triggers her defensiveness and leads to conflict that doesn't get resolved. On rare occasions, however, S.C. shows the fragility that forms the core of her personality structure. What comes through at these times is her sense of her own weakness. It is likely that the fragility of her ego is responsible for her strategy: to be noticed, but not engaged.

Through this view of S.C., the ambivalent underpinnings of abrasive behavior begin to become apparent. This person, appearing untouchable by others' feelings, operates from both a need for and a fear of emotional contact. One begins to see the quality of abrasiveness as a protection against a yearned-for closeness because of an expectation of being injured.

The abrasive person wades in and people push her* away or leave her, and she rarely acknowledges her part in the duet. Since she sees herself as desiring contact, she does not see that she drives people away. Rather, she conceives of herself as the injured party. She lives in a world of mostly believed narcissistic distortions that are very difficult to deal with directly. Direct confrontation provides resistant contact which engages the person's abrasive qualities.

As first seen in therapy, the abrasive woman often presents herself as a rather sympathetic figure. As the relationship intensifies, and she begins to interact with the therapist at a more personal level, her abrasiveness becomes more apparent.

O.M. entered therapy because of difficulty in maintaining intimate relationships with men. She was attracted to men who were emotionally unavailable, and she attempted to wear them down to get the closeness she said she wanted, continuing until she'd either given up or driven them away. Rapidly, she formed a strong attachment to the therapist which she would acknowledge only through very indirect, sometimes sarcastic comments. She often described her abrasive behaviors but would carefully keep from demonstrating these behaviors with her therapist. She also avoided making direct positive statements or requests.

Her abrasiveness in the therapy situation emerged gradually. Once, following the therapist's inability to reschedule an appointment at her request, she became sarcastic and harshly demanding, but later she was able to discuss her hurt and her disappointed feelings about not being cared for sufficiently. Much later, about 2 years into therapy, her abrasiveness became pronounced in relation to two events —a scheduling error and a billing error—that occurred within a

---

*We are discussing women patients from this point on and will use the feminine pronoun.

few weeks of each other. O.M. again became sarcastically demanding, name calling, and insisting on extra sessions because of "the [therapist's] countertransference problems that were affecting [her] therapy." She raged at the therapist for disappointing her and questioned whether the relationship could be salvaged. She clearly had been deeply wounded and frightened by the events.

O.M. had grown up an only child in a family where there was not much nurturance for anyone: Her parents were very self-involved. Her mother had a merged relationship with her, giving her little guidance and never challenging her view of things. Neither parent was willing to stand up to her childhood anger and she reported feeling frightened at the "power" she had. They did not serve as guides to help her channel her narcissistic view of herself and she retained it, expecting the world to react to her as uncritically as did her parents.

For O.M. the therapist, in committing the above described errors, had shifted from being the idealized good mother to being a recapitulation of O.M.'s actual mother: ineffective, uncaring, and potentially life threatening. She felt abandoned in the therapy as she had felt in her family, and her disappointment and fear led her to want to terminate therapy. Her drive to health and the trust established in the prior two years provided sufficient foundation that she was able not to act on her feelings, but rather she worked hard in the ensuing sessions to mend the break.

O.M.'s abrasiveness was a shield against experiencing her feelings of hurt and fear of abandonment. In her family it was an adaptive behavior in response to the ineffectiveness and emotional unavailability of her parents, whom she experienced as careless, helpless, and thus dangerous. Her shield of abrasiveness allowed her to step out into the world quite effectively without too much risk of getting hurt. As people would get closer to her, however, this defense became an impediment to real intimacy. In therapy, she began to feel much of the fear and pain, saw her ability to get through it, and consequently was able to allow much more closeness. At the same time, she began to be able to risk asking directly for things she wanted and to risk expressing anger directly when it arose.

O.M.'s history further exemplified several aspects of the abrasive pattern: (a) While she found the confrontation with her therapist fear and anger producing she was able to persevere in this emotionally difficult situation. For the abrasive person, the self system is hungry, but wounded and in need of protection. However, it also is one that is strong enough to keep striving for nourishment and completion through interaction with people. Still, because of the conflicts previously detailed, these interactions tend to perseverate in self-defeating patterns. (b) She had a good energy stores and was able to function well in the world of work and external achievements. The abrasive women we have observed have generally been high-functioning people of significant academic and/or professional accomplishments. However, since they seem to derive little inner satisfaction from their achievements, this investment in the development of their external resources would seem to be part of their defensive systems rather than simply a healthy expression of ability and growth. (c) She presented for therapy as a result of interpersonal conflicts rather than as a result of inner turmoil. While therapy with abrasive patients eventually illuminates intrapsychic problems, these patients generally present initially with complaints of an interpersonal nature.

These points are further exemplified by the following vignette:

> L.P. was a woman in her early 30s. She came to therapy because of marital difficulties, but before long began to report phobic behaviors, obsessive thoughts, and emotionally related somatic complaints. Her husband was extremely withdrawn and would generally retreat or explode when pursued. L.P. initially denied that she had a role in the interactions leading to this behavior. Typically, as the work would focus on her part in problem situations, she would deflect the therapist's comments, begin to justify herself, and dismiss any attempts to reframe as irrelevant.

> L.P. was quite successful in her profession as well as being an accomplished artist of some repute. Nonetheless, she took little satisfaction from her considerable achievements but used them as a bludgeon when she felt emotionally overwhelmed by others. L.P., typical of the person with this typology, encompassed competence in the external environment as part of the defensive fortifications, both as a way of holding onto a sense of worth and of keeping others within her orbit. She had a diminished sense of her personal value and felt that she needed to let people know of her accomplishments to keep them interested. These accomplishments brought her little inner satisfaction and she'd talk of returning from a successful exhibition of her work feeling empty. She often used her feats as an interpersonal device to convince others of her value, but she did it in such a way that others felt diminished and further distanced themselves.

L.P.'s behavior illustrates the dilemma of people in this abrasive category: The more tender and in need she felt, the more she also felt vulnerable to being damaged with an unconscious assumption that the likelihood of being damaged was high. This conflict got played out in such a way that to be defensive was to become offensive. She therefore elicited self-protective pushing away responses in others especially at those times when she most needed holding, and she guarded against seeing how her behavior engendered this flight in others.

THERAPY

Therapy with the abrasive woman is a long term project and is filled with pitfalls. She does not usually appear as openly angry; there is often, as we have said, a sympathetic quality to her initially, but there is something not quite right. She can present herself as victim, but her strength is quite obvious. As a therapist, one may begin to feel worn down by the sessions unless one can step back and see the whole picture, attend to the inconsistencies, and see the hurt and fear underneath.

There is a difficulty in trying to provide a corrective therapeutic experience to people who, when moved by an inner desire for closeness, engage in distancing maneuvers without acknowledging their behaviors. Because of the tendency of these patients to present themselves as unassailably right and to push away at the first sign of subtotal acceptance, it is important for the therapist to understand the stance and the dilemma of these abrasive patients and to focus the work on the injury and not on the resistance. If the therapist engages the defenses, not only will the patient not benefit, but also will the therapist feel the wear.

The abrasive woman entering therapy presents a great deal to work with. As described above, these patients have a drive toward contact, good energy supplies, and an ability to create and use external resources. Very often they are high-drive achievers and can persevere even in the face of much frustration. The abrasive person has developed good, adaptive defenses in the face of narcissistic, insensitive parenting, and those who present for therapy can often benefit from the experience given a therapist who understands their processes.

The alliance must be made with the wounded, vulnerable aspects of the personality. If the therapist, like others in this patient's environment, attacks the abrasiveness, s/he gets worn down. A way of preventing abrasion for the therapist might be to become harder and more closed, but since the patient's drive is for contact, this would likely either intensify the abrasion or drive the patient away from the perceived rejection. In short, this tactic mirrors the patient's early treatment, and reinforces the pathology rather than providing a corrective experience. A more therapeutic stratagem is to "caress the underbelly," that is, to identify the person's hurt, responding to the attempt at contact rather than to the pushing away.

The abrasive person most often gets met in the world with diminished contact, because others either flee or shut down. As the emotionally involved patient begins to respond more openly, the therapist must be able to see the hurt in his/her patient and to try to focus the patient on it. One must take care not to be too aggressive in providing nurturance, however, since real contact soon becomes overwhelming to this person, and the patient's efforts at distancing must also be respected. As therapy begins, the therapist must also carefully ration any negative feedback about the patient's behavior. The patient's defensive structure rests on a foundation of grandiosity and infallibility. To begin to examine directly any aspect of this person is perceived as a rejection of the whole, and reinforces an inherent sense of their worthlessness in being.

The key to building and maintaining a useful alliance keeps the therapist returning to focus on the perception of the patient as being internally fragile, even though this is denied by the patient. The therapist must provide support for this weakened deep structure initially without acknowledging it. The patient's condition of emotional starvation provides the medium that makes it possible to do so, especially by helping her identify and contact the hurt that gets touched both in therapy and outside and that triggers the abrasive response. For some patients this is long-term work. Well into the therapy process the abrasive woman still flees from contact and expression of most emotions. As the ability to feel and express hurt and sadness eventually emerge, they draw after them the rage that seems to underly the abrasive reflex. With the working through of this anger comes the possibility that the patient can effect the emotional separation that can liberate her from the dreadful dilemma that had previously characterized her emotional life. With this patient, as with most, what is needed from the therapist is an understanding of the emotional process that subtends the undesirable behavior. As the therapist responds to the overt without regard to the dynamics, the patient's feared outcomes tend to come to pass and therapy fails. As, however, the therapist responds to the generative forces and the patient's genuine needs even the juggernaut of the abrasive patient can be halted.

Work with these patients is often intense and it is easy for even an experienced and skilled therapist to get drawn into the struggles occasionally. When this happens there is no doubt that the sensitive therapist will feel the wear that characterizes such interactions with these people. Such an awareness, in fact, can be pathognomonic, and help the therapist perceive the patient more clearly. However, such feelings can also interfere with the therapist's ability to maintain the stance necessary to be therapeutic. In working with these difficult patients, especially at the potentially frustrating early stages, it is of great importance that the therapist have an arena for his/her personal nurturance. Without this—supervision, peer group, and so forth—it is possible that the frustration generated in the work could spill back into the relationship and create problems for the therapist, patient, and their work together.

CODA

Abrasiveness is a powerful metaphor that served to help us conceptualize particular people, particular personality facets, and particular relationships. The positive aspects of abrasiveness need to be kept in mind. Particularly, as therapists, we need to see the potential for aliveness in it; it is an attempt at contact, albeit an ineffective insistence on it. Even though abrasive people present to therapy because of "other people" there is a deep need which they are hoping to have met. Discovering and attending to that is an important way of reaching them.

Treating the Abrasive Client with Rational-Emotive Therapy (RET)

Albert Ellis

Resistant clients are numerous, as the psychotherapeutic literature attests (Wachtel, 1982; Weiner, 1982). I have found, however, that most of them are much more stubborn than they are abrasive, and that the techniques of rational-emotive therapy (RET) that I have recently outlined in detail for use with resistant individuals (Ellis, in press-a, in press-b, 1984) do not necessarily work with some who are particularly irritating. This paper shall therefore be devoted to RET techniques that are especially applicable to this type of client.

One of the main reasons the usual kinds of interpersonal and dialogue methods, such as those commonly used in RET (and in various other therapies) often fail is that abrasive individuals are not only hostile to their relatives and associates but to therapists as well. And they often *enjoy* jousting with and thwarting the therapist. Consequently, they actively fight against the therapist's rational-persuasive teaching and do their best to invalidate them. They also tend to meet therapeutic acceptance and warmth with savage hostility, thus nullifying its effectiveness.

Let me illustrate with the case of one of my most abrasive clients, whom I shall call Abrasa. Although I saw her in individual and group therapy for two years with very poor results, I was finally able to reach her with the use of several cognitive behavioral methods that are sometimes relatively ineffective with other kinds of clients. When I first saw her, Abrasa was 25 years old, a college dropout who seemed to be unemployable and who, in spite of her physical attractiveness and her general interest in males, never dated. She was thoroughly convinced that men were only interested in her body and in her money (because her family was fairly wealthy)—and she let her prospective dates know this within 10 minutes of meeting them at bars and dances. She fought with me continually, insisting that I did not really understand her and was biased against her; and in two of my regular therapy groups, each of which she attended for 6 months, she fought with all the other group members and

Albert Ellis, Ph.D., a 1948 graduate in clinical psychology from Columbia University, is founder and main theoretician of Rational-Emotive Therapy and the Executive Director of the Institute for Rational-Emotive Therapy.

was so obnoxious and hateful that about eight of them quit the group, stating that she disrupted the group process and that they could not get much out of therapy as long as she was in their group. Although several of the group members went out of their way to help her, especially with her problems of relating to people, she rebuffed their efforts and insisted that they disliked her. Eventually, she created a self-fulfilling prophecy, so that they really did dislike her, and some of them asked to have her leave the group.

At one point, she quit the group and chose to have individual therapy with one of the associate male leaders who acted warmly to her and to whom she was sexually attracted. This only lasted for a few sessions, however, because she fell in love with the therapist, insisted that he secretly loved her (although he was happily married and told her frankly that he had no personal interest in her), and bothered him with gifts and with personal telephone calls until he completely refused to see her for further sessions. She then returned to having individual sessions with me (in spite of her personal dislike for me), but she made little progress as they continued and fought vehemently with me almost every session.

Neither I nor her therapy group at first helped Abrasa. We arrived at what we were pretty sure were her main irrational beliefs—especially, "I must have people love me no matter how badly I treat them!" and "I absolutely *need* what I want and the world *must* give me what I need immediately, with no real effort on my part!" But we rarely got her to agree that she devoutly believed these irrationalities; and we certainly never got her, by our active disputing techniques, to surrender them.

I finally did, however, help her to improve significantly in several respects. First, she went back to college, stuck it out for 2 more years, and graduated. Second, she obtained a job as a bookkeeper and worked steadily and well at it. Third, she developed the knack of meeting a number of males and was able to have dates, although no steady relationships. Fourth, for the first time in her life she made a few close women friends. Although she was by no means cured of her anxiety and hostility, she made what for her were remarkable gains.

How were these achieved? By a number of rational-emotive methods, especially these:

Cognitively, I strongly and steadily showed Abrasa how she was defeating herself and I forcefully insisted that she would continue to be a basket case unless she worked hard at changing her ideas and her behavior. I wrote up a long list of the disadvantages of her irritating behavior and gave her the homework assignment of reading this list to herself at least five times a day. "I don't agree with this list," she argued. "What will happen if I don't keep reading and thinking about it?" "You'll damned well suffer—and suffer for the rest of your life!" I replied. She soon started to go over the list.

One of the most effective cognitive methods I used with this client was modeling. The group assigned her to come regularly to my Friday Night Workshop at the Institute for Rational-Emotive Therapy in New York City, where I give demonstrations of RET with members of the public who volunteer to bring up a personal problem in front of an audience of about 100 people. By watching me use RET many times with these volunteers and by actively using it with them herself during the discussion period, Abrasa became quite adept at talking others out of their irrational beliefs; and by doing so on many occasions she unconsciously, without even trying, began to talk herself out of some of her own main irrationalities.

Seeing that she was doing so well talking to the demonstratees at the Friday Night RET workshop, I induced Abrasa to use RET, as well, with her friends and her business associates. Again, she became quite adept at doing so, and helped a number of people who were fairly seriously anxious and depressed. When she later referred some of them to me as clients, I could see that they had already been half-therapized by her and already knew some of the main elements of RET. The technique of encouraging clients to use RET disputing with their relatives and associates is a standard RET procedure (Bard, 1980; Ellis, 1962, 1973; Ellis & Abrahms, 1978). But it seemed to work better than it usually does in Abrasa's case because although she was quite resistant to being talked out of her own irrational Beliefs, she was eager to talk others out of theirs. And doing so seemed to help her considerably.

RET problem-solving methods also worked well with Abrasa. She wanted very practical techniques of getting a job, succeeding at school, and encountering males; and when such techniques were given to her, as they often are given to clients in the course of RET's cognitive practices, she was able to use them effectively. While theoretical discussion had little effect, practical planning to get more of what she wanted in life was quite effective (Ellis, 1984; Ellis & Abrahms, 1978; Grieger & Boyd, 1980; Walen, DiGiuseppe, & Wessler, 1980).

Emotively, I used with Abrasa the usual RET method of accepting her unconditionally, no matter how hostile she behaved toward me, the therapy group, or outsiders. Although I did not pretend to like her and although I often showed her how obnoxious and self-defeating her behavior was, I practically never felt or experienced anger toward her; and I often showed her that though her acts were abhorrent she was never a bad or rotten person—nor were any of the scores of people she kept endlessly damning (Ellis, 1973, 1984; Ellis & Grieger, 1977). Although she first was sure that I totally hated her, she was able to see, by my verbal and nonverbal attitudes, that I only deplored some of her actions without downing or loathing her *self* or her *personhood*.

At first, Abrasa was entirely humorless in her approach to life and to therapy. She did, however, take to some of the rational humorous songs that we often use in RET (Ellis, 1977, 1981) and she particularly enjoyed singing to herself these two songs:

BEAUTIFUL HANGUP (Stephen Foster, Beautiful Dreamer)
Beautiful hangup, why should we part
When we have shared our whole lives from the start?
We are so used to taking one course
Oh, what a crime it would be to divorce!
Beautiful hangup, don't go away!
Who will befriend me if you do not stay?
Though you still make me act like a jerk,
Living without you would take so much work!
Living without you would take too much work!

WHEN I AM SO BLUE (Johann Strauss, Beautiful Blue Danube)
When I am so blue, so blue, so blue
I sit and I stew, I stew, I stew!
I deem it so awfully horrible
That my life is rough and scarrable!
Whenever my blues are verified
I make myself doubly terrified,
For I never choose to refuse
To be blue about my blues!

(Lyrics by Albert Ellis. Copyright 1980 by Institute for Rational-Emotive Therapy)

Behaviorally, Abrasa was given many homework assignments, especially in regard to doing her term papers at school, looking for jobs, and encountering members of the other sex. At first, she refused to do any of them but I and her therapy group kept after her and monitored her regularly until she started to do them under our direction and to gain confidence that she could continue to do them herself. Although reinforcements did not work, at first, to get her to do her homework, setting and checking up on her, employing stiff penalties, soon began to work very well. Thus, she only started to go on job interviews when she burned a $10 bill (or the group burned it for her) every time she promised to arrange such interviews and then copped out on arranging them. And she began to approach males at dances only when she agreed to clean her bathroom for an hour every time she avoided approaching one.

Behavioral rehearsal also worked with Abrasa when other therapy techniques failed. When she was shown, through verbal instruction and role playing, how to approach and talk with members of the other sex, she at first resisted but eventually became unusually adept at picking up attractive males in public places. Being able to talk to them in a friendly, unhostile manner took quite a while longer, but she later improved considerably in that respect, too.

I no longer see Abrasa for therapy, since she now considers herself "cured." But she still attends my Friday Night Workshops regularly and although I think she still has quite a way to go in relating intimately to others, everyone who knows her agrees she is considerably improved—and at least 75% less abrasive. From observing her, as well as quite a few other highly irritating clients I have seen during the past 40 years, I again want to emphasize that because of their unusually argumentative manner, and the fact that they often like defeating others (including therapists) in debating, other kinds of cognitive, emotive, and behavioral methods—such as ones mentioned above—are more suitable for these kinds of clients. If methods like these are strongly and consistently employed, they will still remain D.C.'s (difficult customers). But not necessarily hopeless ones!

REFERENCES

Bard, J. A. (1980). *Rational emotive therapy in practice.* Champaign, IL: Research Press.

Ellis, A. (1962). *Reason and emotion in psychotherapy.* Secaucus, NJ: Lyle Stuart and Citadel Press.

Ellis, A. (1973). *Humanistic psychotherapy: The rational-emotive approach.* New York: Crown.

Ellis, A. (1983). Rational-emotive therapy (RET) approaches to overcoming resistance. 1: Common forms of resistance. *British Journal of Cognitive Psychotherapy, 1* (1), 28-38.

Ellis, A. (in press-a). Rational-emotive therapy (RET) approaches to overcoming resistance. 2: How RET disputes clients' irrational, resistance-creating beliefs. *British Journal of Cognitive Psychotherapy.*

Ellis, A. (in press-b). Rational-emotive therapy (RET) approaches to overcoming resistance. 3. Using emotive and behavioral techniques of overcoming resistance. *British Journal of Cognitive Psychotherapy.*

Ellis, A. (1984). *Rational-emotive therapy and cognitive behavior therapy.* New York: Springer.

Ellis, A., & Abrahms, E. (1978). *Brief psychotherapy in medical and health practice.* New York: Springer.

Ellis, A., & Grieger, R. (Eds.). (1977). *Handbook of rational-emotive therapy.* New York: Springer.

Grieger, R., & Boyd, J. (1980). *Rational-emotive therapy: A skills based approach.* New York: Van Nostrand Reinhold.

Wachtel, P. L. (Ed.). (1982). *Resistance: Psychodynamic and behavioral approaches.* New York: Plenum.

Walen, S. R., DiGiuseppe, R., & Wessler, R. L. (1980). *A practitioner's guide to rational-emotive therapy.* New York: Oxford.

Weiner, M. F. (1982). *The psychotherapeutic impasse.* New York: Free Press.

The Defeating Patient
and Reciprocal Abrasion

Samuel J. Warner

In the development of a science, there emerges, every so often, a combination of concepts which illuminates our world. In the light generated by this combination we are able to perceive meanings that heretofore had escaped us, or remained obscure.

Such, I believe, is the case with the concepts of "defeatism" and "reciprocal abrasion." Let us study their interaction: There may be profit for us not only in our understanding of what takes place in baffling therapy situations, but also in terms of what each of us can actually *do* to deal with related difficult problems of technique.

Let us begin with this candid contribution by Carl Rogers (1983):

> The worst case of my life was a schizophrenic girl whom I dealt with very well at first at Ohio State and she followed me to Chicago. I began to get sort of tired of working with her. I vacillated back and forth between being a good therapist and being someone who just sort of saw her because I had to keep her from becoming psychotic or something. Anyway she began to touch all the painful buttons in me. I thought I was going crazy myself. I remember one of her dreams. She dreamt that she was a cat and she was clawing out the vitals of some person and she really didn't want to. That was a beautiful description of our relationship. She really didn't want to murder me but that is what she was slowly doing. I finally realized I was just going to crack up. Fortunately for me we had a young psychiatrist working with us. One day I told him at lunch that I really wanted him to take over that case and he said, "Okay, how about next week?" And that made me realize how incredibly urgent it was and I said I'm seeing her this afternoon, could he take over then. He began to realize it was urgent too. He did take over and the moment she was in contact with him she had a full-blown psychosis. (pp. 9-10)

Samuel J. Warner, Ph.D., received his doctorate in clinical psychology from the University of Chicago in 1948. He is presently in private practice and is a member of the faculty of the American Institute for Psychotherapy and Psychoanalysis in New York City.

27

Who could have described better the plight of a therapist subjected to prolonged abrasion? And whose personal Armageddon could provide a better illustration? For if a baffling experience of this sort could happen to a Carl Rogers, then you and I can take heart and face our own debacles.

My own early experience with such a patient was so painful that I immediately organized a series of seminars on this subject at the clinic where I was employed.[1] Shortly afterward I wrote a summary of these recorded seminars, then a review of the literature on this variety of patient for publication (Warner, 1954). There followed two books (1957, 1966), papers delivered at professional meetings, papers published (1956, 1974), —and a dozen years of conducting a seminar on this subject at a psychotherapy training institute.[2]

One might say I had been traumatized by this sort of patient; and from what I have learned in the seminars, there are many other therapists who have suffered this very pain. We generally do not have the courage of a Dr. Rogers, so we lick our wounds quietly over the years, and our debacles remain private.

So, let us now go "public" further. What sort of patient is this article about? It is about the *defeatist*. Our thesis is that the abrasion which occurs is secondary to the patient's defeatism, is caused by that defeatism. We shall see that abrasion occurs in the patient too—but this occurs later in the chain of causation—in a reciprocal interaction which becomes tortuous and complicated. There are surely other causes of abrasion in psychotherapy, but we shall concern ourselves only with the abrasion that is caused by defeatism and its consequences.

By way of overview we are going to relate two sorts of concepts in this paper: (1) the defeating patient, and (2) reciprocal abrasion. I believe you will find these two concepts to provide a sort of Rosetta stone that will permit you to make sense out of disturbing happenings in psychotherapy that would otherwise remain tragic mysteries.

And I aim also in this paper to offer you understanding and procedures which can be of practical help to you, should you run into a patient of this sort. Or, if you have already had such an experience, this paper may help you to assimilate it. For if you are like the rest of us, an experience of this variety has probably left you stunned, hurt, and with a psychological wound that refuses to heal.

Let us now define our terms. The dictionary defines abrasion as the "wearing away of the surface." We are going to see how therapy with this sort of patient may produce a wearing away of two sorts: a wearing away

---

[1]This seminar, on "The Controlling Patient," took place in 1953 at the Mental Hygiene Clinic of the Veterans Administration New York Regional Office, where Dr. Gerard Chrzanowski, who was Consultant in Psychiatry, provided most helpful teaching and guidance.

[2]This seminar is conducted at the American Institute for Psychotherapy and Psychoanalysis in New York City, with the course title of "Psychotherapy With Self-Defeatists."

of the surface of the therapist and a similar reciprocal wearing away in the patient. And the two wearings away are causally interrelated.

What do we mean by a defeating patient? The concept itself has been in the literature at least from 1919 on in the writings of Abraham (1927), and in those of Freud (1927) since 1923. It has surfaced in a number of contexts, but mainly in that of the "negative therapeutic reaction" (p. 71), so termed by Freud, which is one in which a patient makes good progress up to a certain point in treatment and then mysteriously sets out to defeat therapy and the therapist.

We note that Dr. Rogers' comment about the "girl whom I dealt with very well at first" fits this temporal feature of the negative therapeutic reaction. But I must confess, at the start, that I do not know for a fact that Dr. Rogers' patient may be classified as defeating; though, on the face of it, someone who is engaged in "clawing out the vitals" of the therapist, and in his slow "murder" seems reasonably so. I hope my assumption is correct: Dr. Rogers' description is just too splendid an illustration to pass up. But if I am incorrect here, I think the paper will have value through our other illustrations and, I am sure, your own past experiences.

While we are on definitions, let me clarify that although my emphasis in this article will be on the abrasion due to the patient's efforts to defeat the therapist, in the therapy situation defeating the therapist means defeating oneself too, since one came to therapy to succeed at it. Therefore there will be a certain amount of interchangeability of the terms *defeating, self-defeating,* and *self-and-other defeating.*

Now, what are the symptoms, the manifestations of defeating that others have reported? Abraham (1927) saw it in obstructionism in therapy—as in only "pretended compliance" (p. 310). For Horney (1936) there was a "complete refusal to cooperate" and rather efforts "to humiliate the analyst" (p. 36). Bergler (1947) reported "concentrated malice": "He is intent on squeezing you out, and waits silently till you exhaust yourself" (p. 72). Chrzanowski (1978) stated, "Such patients have a particular faculty to turn everything therapeutically useful into ashes" (p. 410). The signs are many: Clearly, they reported, such a patient operates *to defeat.*

And *why* does the patient do something as outlandish as defeating the very therapy and the therapist he or she had hoped would afford help? These dynamics of defeating have been dealt with in scattered places of the literature covering hostility, power, guilt, anxiety, vengeance, pride, significance, and a number of other factors and interactions. These have been outlined in my prior publications, and it would lead us afield to describe them here. What suffices for our discussion is this elemental formulation: The patient *defeats* because it is his or her way of getting needed emotional satisfactions. In the hierarchy of defenses, defeating others has a high and prominent position.

THE SPECIAL SIGNIFICANCE OF DEFEATING

"Well now," you might say, "why the fuss about this defeating patient? After all, each and every one of us does various things in order to achieve emotional satisfactions. Why single out defeatism for such special consideration?"

And that is a major point of this paper: *If you are working with a patient who defeats in order to get basic emotional satisfactions, then you are in a situation which is qualitatively different from working with other sorts of patients.*

We are going to see why such a patient is different, in terms of the effect on the therapist. We shall see that the term *abrasive* is particularly helpful to describe this effect.

We shall see that this abrasion in the therapist produces a counterabrasion in the defeating patient in complex and complicated ways: This counterabrasion may have most serious consequences for the course of therapy and the patient's mental health.

We shall see why the problems posed by the defeating patient will not go away by themselves. When there is ultimate failure with other sorts of patients, some "civilized" termination is usually possible, with mutual agreement. Not so with the defeatist. We shall understand why difficulties in reciprocal abrasion with defeating patients often escalate to the insurmountable, with an ending that is painful and traumatic.

Therefore, we can sense why the therapist working with a defeating patient has a special need for understanding what is going on, and a special need for grasping the techniques that might be helpful in working with such a patient. And it is to that understanding and that grasp that we now address ourselves.

The key to understanding the problem of the defeating patient resides in this paradox: The essential meaning of defeating someone, for this sort of patient, is that it is a mechanism of defense, a way of defending oneself against anxiety; but it is also, ipso facto, a way of creating new (and perhaps worse) anxiety.

There are two clear technical implications of this paradox. The first is standard textbook dictum: Because the one who defeats is frightened and anxious, you the therapist must extend yourself to understand him or her so as to help deal with the anxiety. But the second is less well appreciated, even controversial, as we shall later see: Because the defeating operations can cause so much trouble, you the therapist must do all you can to prevent their being acted out excessively, lest therapy fall victim to reciprocal abrasion.

How can therapy fall victim to reciprocal abrasion? Well, the first step with this sort of patient, is the acting out of the defeatism. What the patient does may not amount to anything much, at first. He or she may come late repeatedly, may linger at the door prior to leaving, may spend a few extra minutes in the bathroom so that sessions begin late. The patient may be slow in paying the bill, or may sass you with passive-aggressiveness, refusing to see the point you have taken pains to make —quite masterfully, of course.

I can sense the reader demurring, "My heavens, Dr. Warner. Since when did pettiness in a therapist become good technique? I *had* thought permissiveness in a therapist was a better thing!"

Yes, attention to such details does appear petty. But you must bear this in mind. Such defeatism registers in the patient; it is very important to him or her. It is not petty—deep within the person. Every minor victory of this sort over the therapist says to the person, "You are *powerful*. Look how you were able to manipulate your therapist. And *fool* him!"

And so, our patient—who has just defeated you in some seemingly petty way—feels powerful. It is ancient wisdom that the powerful need not be afraid. If you want the thesis developed with genius you can look into Karen Horney's (1936) extensive treatment of the alternation of love and power as defenses, and Nietzsche's (1924) two volumes on *The Will to Power*. Enough? We will accept that your patient feels, for the moment, less afraid, less anxious because he or she has been able to manipulate you destructively, to defeat you in some way, however minor.

But whom has the patient defeated? Only the one who symbolizes the parent of childhood, perhaps of infancy. Only, therefore, the most powerful magician in the world. True, the patient may not verbalize this, may not be aware of this. But deep down she or he knows of succeeding in committing an aggression against the very one to whom he or she has come in desperation for critically needed help.

And so the patient starts to become anxious again. What to do to head it off? Why not use the method that "worked" last time—manipulate your therapist? Why not phone—without a really good need for it? Why not be "dense" while you are talking to the therapist, who probably won't catch on, and who will take you as deadly serious. Say there's some emergency; that you've *got* to talk on the phone right away. And then, the next scheduled session—come late!

With each petty aggression, with each defeat of what the patient knows the therapist wants and wants him or her to do, a "victory" is garnered, a brief respite from anxiety is enjoyed. But there is a spiraling effect: because, as the patient proves the therapist's feet are of clay, he or she loses more and more an important defense: respect for therapy and the therapist—and anxiety's plateau moves higher.

And in time, the element of abrasion rears its ugly head. For no one likes to be manipulated destructively, to have one's will thwarted, to be rendered powerless—and we therapists resent it. Our good teacher Rogers (1983) said of his patient: "She began to touch all the painful buttons in me" (p. 10). Our protective layer over these buttons gets worn away by our being defeated, repeatedly, repeatedly—even in relatively small ways. We become angry. We try to control the anger. We try not to show it. We repeat to ourselves that a good therapist is permissive. And we want to be, truly to be, good therapists.

All this is not wasted on our patient, who is tuned in to our distress far more than is revealed. And it is upsetting because, he or she wants to be a good patient and wants us to be a good therapist. The patient does hope to get benefit from therapy, truly, but is unhappy and anxious in the here and now. What to do? Of course. Defeatism is deeply ingrained as a mechanism of defense: It *does* make one feel better, in the short run.

And so, we have a vicious circle of cause and effect. The patient's defeating operations wear away the usual professional "skin," and expose the "buttons" that become easier to press. We may not all feel we are going insane over it, but we can become extremely upset, disturbed.

The vicious circle, the spiraling, also has an abrasive effect on the patient. Regression is, after all, a clear principle of adjustment. The patient who finds his or her world becoming increasingly difficult, may slip back to a slightly lower level of defenses and, for the time being, may experience a little less anxiety.

And as the patient regresses, the therapist may note, with some alarm, that the patient is doing less-"appropriate" things. These are still the same sorts of things: but he or she comes a little later, lingers longer before leaving, combing hair "just right" takes a few minutes longer in the bathroom, cuts a few minutes more off the session, and so on. Nothing gross, yet; but somehow anxiety starts to seep into the consciousness of the therapist who isn't quite sure why, but senses something is wrong.

And so, the spiraling may continue. Further anxiety leads to further defeatism, to temporary relief, then deeper anxiety, and further defeatism—this time on a little more regressed level. And in all this the bewildered therapist may cling to "permissiveness"—as a captain of a ship clings to his honor as it sinks and his cap floats slowly off his head.

Where the patient's apparent personality represented a rather thin system of defenses covering over a psychotic personality organization (as has been described in the literature under "pseudoneurotic forms of schizophrenia") then the emergence of frank psychosis is the readier. There, the abrasion in the patient has reached its ultimate: The adaptive levels have been worn away. And I wonder how many therapists have also fallen victim to this abrasion, to the very same extent. How many have really gotten sick over it, or left the profession?

CONSIDERATIONS OF TECHNIQUE

So? What can we, as therapists, do about it?

I have summarized the various elements of technique set forth in the literature for dealing with the defeating patient in three published places mentioned earlier, so there is little need to do the same here. What there *is* substantial need for, however, is to zero in on the two dimensions of abrasion, and to present the central elements of orientation which a therapist must grasp in order to avoid this reciprocal abrasion into pathology, and handle the defeating patient constructively.

These central elements of orientation may be difficult to grasp, for it offends us to think that a human being could come to us for treatment, and then set out to defeat us. And so we want to deny it; we resent having to grasp it, to acknowledge it. I remember taking a brilliant and usually gracious professor to dinner shortly after I had written my first paper in this area, and she said to me something she had apparently given much thought to: "If you *really* believe that there is such a thing as a defeating patient, then perhaps you shouldn't be doing therapy *at all!*"

By strange coincidence, there is an addendum to this story: About 25 years later a young man came to me for treatment, explicitly because, as he said, he was a self-defeatist. And when, in giving the background, he said he had been in treatment with the professor in the prior paragraph, and I murmured interest, he said, "Oh yes! I drove her back to smoking!"

"Really," I said. "And how did you do that?"

"Oh," he replied, "I was in her group—and she had just made an interpretation about somebody in the group—and I quietly said, 'I don't think that's *true!*' I used to do that to her. And she looked blank. And then she jumped up and bolted oùt of the room, and came back in a few seconds—puffing wildly at a cigarette. And she hadn't smoked for months before this!"

Accordingly, if you want to deal adequately with a defeating patient, the first step is *to believe*, to accept that there *is* such a thing as a defeating patient. And as I have indicated, for many, this is not easy to do.

Next, seek to understand the phenomenon of defeatism. It will be a strain: Nietzsche grew mad as he applied his genius to structuring this problem; it will take you to very unflattering and unsavory levels of human nature. But you must understand, if you are to be a constructive force with this problem.

Next, learn to recognize the defeatism for what it is—as quickly and as effectively as possible. For time is an important dimension of treatment: If the therapist is deceived into believing that the defeating behavior is really something else—some harmless or innocent expression—then, by the time he or she "gets wise," the therapy situation may have passed the point of no return, sliding into oblivion.

It is true, as Reich (1949) pointed out, that one must permit (what he termed) the "psychoanalytic personality" (p. 27) to emerge *before* one intervenes incisively in the flow of process; and yet the prior consideration of timing is critical. If you recognize defeatism for what it is early in therapy (Abraham, 1927; Durkin, 1957; Horney, 1936), you may be able to confront the patient with it while it is yet a relatively minor gambit, one he or she can analyze constructively. But if you wait too long, repetition, regression, and cumulative reciprocal abrasion may render that defeating operation much less susceptible to constructive analysis, much more likely to be an instrument of abrasion that persists rigidly in accelerating effect.

Next, you must be prepared to *do* something about the defeatism; and you must learn *what* to do. There are many categories of patients who require little more than an accepting milieu in therapy, and who thrive beautifully in it. Not so with defeating patients: If you do not actively do something sufficient about them, then the sort of trauma that Dr. Rogers described—and many other therapists, including myself have endured—will be yours. And it will be painful.

So, now, assuming you are convinced that you must *do something*. What? Probably the best single treatise on technique with self-defeatists is Wilhelm Reich's (1949) historic paper, "The Masochistic Character," published originally in 1932, and then as a chapter of his *Character Analysis*. Of course, Horney, Bergler, Reik, and many others have contributed substantially to elements of applicable technique, but Reich's is probably the most comprehensive treatment of the self-defeatist (or as he termed it, "masochist" [p. 223]). His treatment, of course, is in the context of character analysis, with its many and subtle parameters.

The central element of what you do, that I want to stress in this paper, is helping defeatists to become aware that they are defeating, helping them to be an object to themselves sufficiently to perceive that they actually do things to frustrate and ineffectualize the therapist. This is, of course, difficult to do; and the voluminous considerations of "analysis of resistance" enter.

Yet I want to make this central point clear. You, the therapist dealing with self-defeatists must help them to become aware of their defeatism: you must not ignore it, hoping it will go away by itself. It won't. It will, in all probability, get worse—in line with the two reciprocal dimensions of abrasion we discussed.

It is *not* reassuring to such persons if you "accept" their defeatism as good, desirable behavior. Deep within, they know it is not. If you accept this behavior, then they feel rejected as persons; for they deeply feel that if you, omniscient parent, really took them seriously, then you would comprehend what was going on.

They find far more reassurance in your confronting them with what they are doing that is really *un*acceptable. One very large young man, early in my career, who had worked his way through nine therapists in a brief period, put his feet on my desk in our first session and asked to borrow some money (because he had left home without enough). A "polite" therapist would shortly have become number 10, and the search begun for number 11. I must admit that it came naturally to me to observe that I could hardly see over his big feet; and that his using therapy as a banking institution didn't feel right, and was something we should look into. He was not put off by the confrontation. He analyzed rather than acted out; he subsequently made great progress, and later sent his wife for treatment with me, so she could catch up.

This is the element of technique that the masters (Abraham, 1927; Bergler, 1947; Horney, 1936; Reich, 1949) are most in agreement on: that as long as defeatism exists, it should be central to the work, in what is discussed, interpreted, analyzed. There will be *many* things going on, and brought up for discussion by the defeatist, but the masters counsel: Do not be deflected by cajoling or tears; as long as defeatism exists in the session, zero in on it, and subject it to your full armamentarium of analysis—the confrontation, interpretation, and so forth. Reich (1949) tells of lying down on the floor and rolling around to make his point; some (Tabachnik, 1964) threaten termination of treatment; others (Rivière, 1936) assume unusual responsibilities. The specific techniques are many, but they involve this central dictum: that as long as defeatism exists in the therapy session, you, the therapist, keep the existence of this defeatism clearly at the forefront of your awareness, and that you seek, as best you can, to *do something* about it.

That *something* must reflect every bit of sophistication you can marshal. Defeatists are difficult to work with. What may seem to be a relatively small error may make the difference between success and failure with such a patient. Edmund Bergler (1947) has left us a legacy on this point: where the patient pleads for love and yet does things to undermine and destroy whatever love you bear him or her, deal with the latter—this he underlined in many papers and books. To deal with the need for love will make for many pleasant sessions while the patient sets you up for the ultimate defeat; but if you can zero in on, stay with, and eventually analyze the need to destroy the love he or she professes to be seeking, you will have many unpleasant sessions, but the termination may be splendid.

Limits are to a therapist what a compass and the stars are to a navigator (Bixler, 1949). Observing the limits is important in every instance of therapy; but with a defeating patient they are the sine qua non. They are the touchstone against which the patient's behavior must be tested regularly. However weird and wild are a patient's verbalizations, as long as he or she observes the limits—comes on time, leaves on time, and so on—the therapist can feel reasonably secure that progress is "on course." On the other hand, however "proper" the verbalizations of a patient—if his or her behavior breaks limits, an alarm should ring in the therapist's head. And the more defeating the patient, the louder the alarm. For few things can be so abrasive to a therapist as the regular and repeated breach of limits.

Therefore, especially with the defeating patient, care must be taken that the limits are observed. Where they are not, such breaches must be picked up for analysis, and care taken to assimilate their dynamic and developmental grounds. Where limits continue to be broken, more intensive efforts at analysis are immediately called for. And where all efforts at analysis fail, and the violations persist, warning of termination must be given; and if this proves insufficient, actual termination must be effected.

Hopefully, aid will be extended to the patient in the matter of finding another therapist. But if the patient acts so as to defeat you in the "proper" termination too, then termination must be effected as best you can, giving the names and phone numbers of institutes that maintain panels of fully trained therapists. For it is severely destructive to maintain a crippled relationship after it has ceased to be constructive. It makes for further (and severe) abrasion in the therapist; and, in line with spiraling, for crippling abrasion in the patient. And the end result of this mutual and reciprocal abrasion can be the emergence of frank psychosis.

Therefore you should—through reading, seminars, and pointed observation—seek to become knowledgeable and sophisticated about the various patterns of self-and-other defeat so that you can recognize each most expeditiously and be in a position to do something effective as soon as is feasible rather than being sucked into a swift current of reciprocal abrasion. If you know what to look for, you can perceive it more quickly.

I wish I could say there is unanimity of opinion on these prior points in the literature. We love neat solutions. But there are those who take a diametrically opposing view with regard to key dimensions (Berliner, 1947, 1958; Eisenbud, 1967; Rogers & Haigh, 1983). In dealing with defeatists, they say, there is nothing worse than to stress the defeatism: rather, you should comprehend their need for love, and seek to share a reasonable measure of it with them. And as to timing, they counsel caution, rather than picking up the defeatism for analysis as soon as its presence is substantial.

I must confess that I lean toward the prior or "hard" position, rather than this latter "soft" one. I have devoted a paper (1974) to these dilemmas you and I face when in the presence of defeatists: to be hard or soft with them. I sense there is merit to both views, depending on the situation: You would have to be softer with someone of low ego strength—a person on the verge of a breakdown. You would want to wait as long as you could, very early in treatment, to first get the feel of what is really going on. Surely, you would like to wait until enough of a relationship has been established, so that the patient could feel that your confrontation or interpretation (which is bound to be substantially ego-alien) came from a heart that wished him or her well.

And I wish you well, young therapists embarking on the rough seas of defeatism, where we older ones have sought to navigate and have sometimes foundered. And when you have a moment you might reflect on the interaction of reciprocal abrasion and defeatism in the larger social scene: For many of us may profess to be constructive, and yet, in truth, if you look closely, you may find that experiences in life have worn away constructive attitudes so that nihilism is really being served. Nietzsche (1924) was brave enough, later in life, to admit that for all his "superman" preachings he was "a Nihilist from top to toe." And we? Is social living wearing away constructive attitudes in many of us, too? And are we unconsciously seeking to defeat life in society? Are the essential phenomena represented by littering and graffiti limited to the obvious bitterness of the underprivileged, worn away by interaction with a society they have grinding difficulty living in? Or are more serious results of reciprocal abrasion in process of becoming manifest in the larger social scene, produced by brighter and more affluent members of society, whose inner dreams have yet been worn away by life, too? I made a stab at finding answers here a quarter of a century ago (Warner, 1956, 1957). In our thermonuclear age these may be important questions for you younger social scientists to ponder.

REFERENCES

Abraham, K. (1927). A particular form of neurotic resistance against the psychoanalytic method. *Selected papers on psychoanalysis*. London: The Hogarth Press.

Bergler, E. (1947). Specific types of resistance in orally regressed neurotics. *The Psychoanalytic Review, 34*(1), 58–75.

Berliner, B. (1947). On some psychodynamics of masochism. *Psychoanalytic Quarterly, 16*, 459–471.

Berliner, B. (1958). The role of object relations in moral masochism. *Psychoanalytic Quarterly, 27*, 38–56.

Bixler, R. (1949). Limits are therapy. *Journal of Consulting Psychology, 13*, 1–11.

Chrzanowski, G. (1978). Malevolent transformation and the negative therapeutic reaction. *Contemporary Psychoanalysis, 14*, 405–414.

Durkin, H. E. (1957). Some techniques for the clinical management of masochism. *American Journal of Orthopsychiatry, 27*, 185–199.

Eisenbud, R. (1967). Masochism revisited. *The Psychoanalytic Review, 34*(1), 58–75.

Freud, S. (1927). *The ego and the id*. London: The Hogarth Press.

Horney, K. (1936). The problem of the negative therapeutic reaction. *Psychoanalytic Quarterly, 5*, 29–44.

Nietzsche, F. W. (1924). The will to power. In O. Levy (Ed.), *Complete works*, Part 1, Vol. 14 (p. 22). New York: Macmillan.

Reich, W. (1949). *Character analysis*. New York: Orgone Institute Press.

Riviere, J. (1936). A contribution to the analysis of the negative therapeutic reaction. *International Journal of Psycho-Analysis, 17*, 304–320.

Rogers, C., & Haigh, G. (1983). I walk softly through life. *VOICES: The Art & Science of Psychotherapy, 19*(4), 6–14.

Tabachnick, N. (1964). Failure and masochism. *American Journal of Psychotherapy, 18*, 304–316.

Warner, S. J. (1954). The problem of the "defeating patient" in psychotherapy. *American Journal of Psychotherapy, 8*, 703–718.

Warner, S. J. (1956). The concept of Satan as an aid to the understanding of human destructiveness. *The Journal of Religious Thought, 13*, 93–109.

Warner, S. J. (1957). *The urge to mass destruction.* New York: Grune & Stratton.
Warner, S. J. (1966). *Self-realization and self-defeat.* New York: Grove Press.
Warner, S. J. (1974). *Technical dilemmas with self-defeatists.* New York: Bleuler Psychotherapy
    Center.

Bread from Stones

Richard Kitzler
James Lay

Abrasive patients are not problems in themselves but more often are the cause of problems in others, specifically an existential problem for the therapist which, on analysis, is a lack of faith.

Our task is to present a structural analysis of the here-and-now field interaction that is often labeled "abrasive." However, there is an immediate problem with the label. To talk of an abrasive patient presents the same problem as talking of the seductive patient, the boring patient, or the intimidating patient. The patient can never be viewed in isolation whether within or outside of therapy. There has to be another person to be seduced, bored, or intimidated, etc. There is a field with at least two people, a context, and an interaction. And the instant you begin a detailed analysis of the present experience of abrasiveness, moment by moment, within the therapy session, labels become irrelevant.

With a structural approach to therapy, diagnosis is not separate from treatment. Use of labels is often a well-intentioned redefining of the focus of the work in order to get on at all. Redefinitions such as diagnosis and abrasiveness energize and suspend ignorance in a kind of Brownian psychological movement which interrupts that process of structural analysis and resulting contact, which is treatment. We are now circling the problem of faith: We must throw down our linguistic crutches and immediately walk with the elementary and only tools of therapy: patient *and* therapist *and* the present. Query: Where then is abrasiveness? (This question gets us ineluctably to the problem of a phenomenological description of irrelevance and its importance in therapy. However we will not take up this issue in this paper.)

For heuristic purposes we are forced to initially use these labels in order to finally indicate their tertiary nature. We will take "abrasive" to mean a classic wearing down as in the sense of stones grinding. What is happening in a patient-therapist field to produce this feeling of ball bust-

Richard Kitzler, M.A., is a Fellow and member of the faculty of the Gestalt Institute of New York. He maintains a practice in New York City.

James Lay, Ph.D., completed his studies in clinical psychology at the Florida State University and trained at the Gestalt Institute of New York.

ing? On inspection there appear to be two types of situations that produce this feeling:

Situation 1. From the therapist's viewpoint, the patient is seen as whining, complaining, sulking, brooding, meandering, pseudo-stupid, and/or merely provoking. From the patient's viewpoint, the therapist is seen as tough, demanding, disapproving, and/or impatient.

Situation 2. From the therapist's viewpoint, the patient is seen as habitually combative, stubborn, controlling, refusing to cooperate or to take risks, or refusing to honor the boundaries of the therapeutic role. From the patient's viewpoint, the therapist is seen as too silent or passive, wrong, or lacking courage to step out of narrow roles.

The adjectives used above are words descriptive of aggression, felt or avoided. The problem consequently seems to be primarily a lack of contactful aggression within the patient-therapist field. In our view the patient as well as the therapist avoids this contact. The patient avoids due to their well-perceived anguish that is anticipated. But why does the therapist avoid contact? The usual reasons given are: (a) There will be storms of emotion that the therapist will not be able to endure; (b) The patient will be driven out of therapy; or (c) The patient's ego is too fragile and will fall apart. (We have the feeling that much of what is called borderline theory is precisely this problem of avoidance of contactful aggression misconceived.)

So in order to get anywhere at all and to prevent anything catastrophic, the therapist typically searches around for concepts to guide his or her work. One approach is to use another set of constructs, in this case sadomasochism. It could be said that the above two ways of experiencing abrasiveness are two examples of a sadomasochistic clinch. Through use of these constructs, what does the therapy gain? Perhaps nothing. A closer look at the dynamics of sadomasochism will hopefully reveal its irrelevance in the actual work of therapy.

Both masochism and sadism are essentially the exercising of a fixed hostility against the self. "To the extent that the aggression is kept inward, there is a well-behaved masochism; to the extent that it [the self] finds some environmental image of itself, there is a fixed sadism" (Perls, Hefferline, & Goodman, 1951, pp. 345–346). In both cases the primary source of the hostility toward the self is an unwanted excitation which is habitually kept unaware. In the case of the sadist, as excitation increases, tension is released by striking, stabbing, and so forth. This striking out is the form in which the sadist desiringly touches the therapist, and the felt gain for the sadist is the increment of excitement released by letting up on the self. Alternatively, for the masochist, as excitement increases there is a parallel increase in restriction, and "the longing for release is neurotically interpreted as the wish to have it done to one, to be forced, broken, punctured, to let loose the inward pressures" (p. 346). The masochist provokes the therapist; and if successful in precipitating a "therapeutic" attack, "loves the brutal [therapist] who gives the underlying release and yet is identified with the self-punishing self" (p. 346).

But how does the therapy proceed with this information? All too often the therapist senses, correctly, that the sadomasochistic behavior has hidden motives and is basically a test. The therapist tries to identify specifically what the test is and then tries to find some way to move through the patient-constructed labyrinth without unproductive bewilderment. The therapist role is traditionally defined around techniques to avoid the traps. As a result the patient is increasingly drawn out on a limb so that hopefully the patient's projections fall of their own weight. The patient then lands in the safety of the positive transference.

A central question may now be asked. Is the above an accurate picture of the process of therapy? Our position is that while it accurately describes much of what is traditionally known as therapy and is indeed good work, it is basically an analysis of the figures of the session and not an analysis of the figure-background structure. Such a procedure is itself falling for a different trap on a more fundamental level and accounts for much of the unaware debilitating consuming of the therapist known as burnout. The therapist is ground up in the above procedure because there is not enough room for the therapist's *self* in what is in fact a therapist-patient field.

In the absence of a structural analysis of the field, the figure-oriented therapy can wear on ad infinitum with much good work and many insights, but we submit that real growth occurs only in the suffering and aware aggression inherent in the step-by-step work that originally goes into creating those figures rather than the figures themselves. We are here talking about the close description and examination of the strengthening of the self, which is not the figure that is created but the creating of the figure.

We have carried on this discussion on what seems to be a theoretical level, but let us give an example.

H. is a 20-year-old who has been seen long enough that the neighbors know the hours of her appointments. The neighbors loiter on the stoops across the street until she enters the therapist's office-apartment. Then they rush across the street and sit on the stoop of the therapist's brownstone and wait for the uproar to begin. On this day H. walks in, stands, stares at the therapist, and with no preparation whatsoever, screams at the top of her lungs: "You hate me! You hate me! You hate me!" Blood-curdling shrieks.

In the therapist's head, with a spasm of fear, the ever-present thought of eviction trembles. He fights down his fear realizing it is pure projection based on New York City's insane rent laws. He cannot help himself wondering what the neighbors will think. Taking a deep breath he resolutely sticks his fingers in his ears and waits for a gap. When she stops for breath finally, he very quietly says, "No. You do not hate me."

This is like a red flag to a bull, and she starts all over again, if anything with a heightened crescendo. You can hear the neighbors outside reassuring the police radio car that everything is all right for the umpteenth time.

Again a pause, then again: "No. You do not hate me. You love me."

You could ask, how is this analysis of structure? How is this different from merely making an interpretation? It is different in that you are stating what is the nature of the patient-therapist relationship as felt by the therapist. You're there and the patient's there and has been and keeps coming back. And that present urgent ongoingness is the nature of the relationship. The patient's hostile behavior is really testing behavior to get herself thrown out because she can't really trust her dependency on you. She feels that she is on the one hand either hopelessly excluded or on the other hand completely swallowed up. Some object, however, to such a direct statement by the therapist on the basis that it pushes the patient toward her fear of being swallowed up. The therapist here is doing the opposite. He is addressing *her*, not her manipulation that would get herself swallowed up again. Her manipulations are aimed at getting herself reassured, held, stroked, or more reliably on the other hand getting herself yelled at and punished. She tries to *be* included by *getting* included. Instead of boundaries that function as a flexible, interactive membrane, she has constructed rigid walls. Instead of reassurance or punishment the therapist quietly states descriptively his felt, experienced interaction. This is to do all you can be at that moment, at that level, with that patient in that state.

The patient in response shrieks, "Aieeeeeeee!"

The therapist puts his fingers in his ears and waits. He shows he will not hear this and that he feels that her shrieks are exaggerated, though serious. When there is a break in the storm, he can didactically address her along the lines, "Now you have said with some force, 'I hate you.' Is this a serious proposition? Because if you are serious, then we will have to address ourselves seriously to it."

The patient replies, "I'm here because I'm desperate. To go to someone else is too much trouble. I can't face starting all over again. I do hate you. You could be more reasonable."

Therapist: "I don't feel that at all. I feel the first part, yes, your despair; but I also feel that you are here and I am here and let's see where we can go from there. Because if you really are serious and your being here is a sum of negatives, then I don't see where we get building on negatives. And I philosophically can't accept that as a human endeavor. And further I'm wondering how really successful you are not only with your words but with your tone in engaging people in your quarrel. God knows there are enough people in the world to punish you if you want to be punished."

Patient: "What is it you think I would say if I was serious?"

Therapist: "I think you would say you love me and perhaps too much."

Patient: "You're just like him! You're just like him! When I started screaming at him, he said you're going to get us evicted, and then I really let him have it."

The manipulative part, the "getting included," the defense of the introjections, the proliferation of false figures, the reaction formations that are defended as attacks on the body if even addressed, are all specious. The thing to do is to support what you feel to be the real field or structural issues: the desperate effort to love you and to be loved in return—"love" in the sense of inclusion—in the only way that they know how to do it. Then move from there into an educative method which is the method of teaching by example and perhaps the dialectical method of Socrates.

Therapist: "I was interested that while you rather forcefully attacked me, there were tears in your eyes. And far from feeling any attack, when I noticed your tears, I myself was feeling sad."

What does it mean for a therapist to reveal more of himself in the therapy? It does not mean that you confess your life to the patient. That is silly and irrelevant. If a patient asks a personal question, the following may be an illustrative reply: "I don't quite see the meaning of this for you in the here and now. Is that really your serious question in the sense that this is information that you need right now or should we ask where it comes from? What is the background for it? Your question is the figure. What is the background? I promise to answer your question if we conclude that you need the answer."

Many conscientious therapists are concerned about allowing too much of themselves into a therapy session because of fear or projecting their own rage or hostility into a session. This problem of the therapist projecting his or her own anger and rage and so forth arises out of the misconceived notion of the therapist revealing himself or herself and the way in which he or she does it. There is no reason for the therapist to be seduced, become angry, bored, or irritated except within a larger context which is *the* background of a very aware (bored) foreground: part of the total picture which is being offered at that point as a contribution to the field —that more enlarged field that the patient must need to understand is also going on. Thus the patient is entitled to know that within the larger field the therapist is feeling seduced, angry, bored, frustrated; but not that the therapist's feeling is all of it or even a big part of it. The therapist can now ask, "What precisely is going on here and now for this feeling to occur?"

But what if the therapist's feeling does take over and is more than just part of the background? Then this is evidence of unfinished business on the part of the therapist which the therapist must submit to a structural analysis. Contrary to the opinion of many, the therapist can submit his or her feeling to a structural analysis in the session with the patient without overburdening the patient and without revealing irrelevant information about the therapist. The rhetoric of revelation must not only be a statement of what is going on but must also be an example of a field statement. The words themselves must also take their place in a hierarchy that also teaches how one speaks field structure. For example,

> I notice in myself that I feel a real interest in your situation at the moment. You seem to me to be using words which don't make a statement of the way I seem to see you, sort of code words. And I notice a little flicker of irritation on my part that you can't make the right words, at least in my view, that would say what you are feeling. Do you now experience what you are saying? Is this what you mean? Because if you do, then we have to address my ignorance in it. And although I would like to go on, just now I can't get past this. I feel stuck here.

There is therefore no need for the therapist to burden himself or herself with pent-up feeling, except through a lack of faith in the therapeutic process. In fact it is a disservice to the patient to omit such an important source of therapeutic awareness. The difficulty for the therapist is that his or her words and rhetoric must constantly reinforce a structural analysis of the field. That is of course the problem in writing this paper.

REFERENCE

Perls, F., Hefferline, R., & Goodman, P. (1951). *Gestalt therapy*. New York: Dell.

Rocks and Glaciers (and Psychosis) "A Wearing Away, as of Rocks by Glaciers. . . ."

Barbara Jo Brothers

I really still want to forget her, just forget her. It has been 4 years? Five? But I don't think she's gone. I catch myself looking twice at small green compact cars even though I remember her saying she's had to get rid of her car. I think I'll hear from her again down the road. Although I have invested volumes of myself in other suicidal patients, wanting them alive, wanting them whole, wanting them to see Life's Potential, I confess I would be relieved to read or hear of Alicia's death. This is not characteristic of me. I consider myself on the end of the scale as having the widest range of tolerance for annoying, irritating behavior of any therapist I know. Hallucinations in my office aren't something with which I can't cope. I've never been attacked by a patient; I think I know how to gauge rage that well. Simpler levels of obnoxious behavior seem to me to be rather clear messages of the depth of a patient's misery and I am generally able to respond therapeutically.

Alicia was different.

Her initial presentation belied what was to come. She was neatly dressed in navy blue and white. She had a large, squarish frame, but was not unattractive in appearance. Her hair was well kept. She was clearly somewhat above average in intelligence, within the bright normal range. She seemed desperate on the telephone and there was an undertone of hostility when she talked about her former therapy, but her mood and affect seemed to me to fall generally within the range of appropriate for a person experiencing anxiety and making a first contact with a therapist. I'm not sure at what point I began to conclude that the anxiety was generated out of psychosis, but I did not register that awareness as a "king-sized problem." I had worked in the state hospital and in state mental health clinics for nearly 10 years. Mere psychosis was no real big deal; I do quite well with schizophrenics anyway.

Once more, Alicia was different.

Barbara Jo Brothers, M.S.W. from Tulane University in 1965, is a licensed social worker now in full-time practice of individual and group psychotherapy.

The colleague from whom I had received this referral had never sent me a patient before this one. I knew this colleague did not, by any means, have a full schedule and I knew he had masochistic leanings. Looking back, this should have been my first clue. But apparently I was so engaged in the appeal to my omnipotence that I disregarded what I will never disregard again. Alicia was piteously telling me this therapist was refusing to see her, had terminated her against her will. She sounded like a weary, burdened 12-year-old. She didn't know what to do. She did not have a lot of money; she was not working full time. I suggested her local mental health center. They wouldn't see her either. In fact, they had called the police the last time she tried to see one of her former therapists there. It seemed to me this could not be legal. Wasn't the state ultimately responsible for the mental health of such individuals? It had certainly seemed so when I was employed in the public sector. Alicia sounded so wearily desperate. As much as I know, intellectually, about rescuer-persecutor-victim triangles, nevertheless, I agreed to see her. Thinking I knew about such dynamics, I thought I could "handle it."

In clock time, Alicia and I didn't last very long together . . . something like April through mid-June. After the first month, I began to understand what Alicia had meant when I asked why the mental health center had called the police and why my colleague refused to see her. I had said, "Were they scared of you, Alicia?", "Had you done something so that they considered you dangerous?"

"No," said Alicia, "I think I just worried them to death."

It seems that Alicia would come to her sessions, presenting herself in a fairly reasonable fashion, and, between her sessions, Alicia would make telephone calls. Not just a couple of times during the week, she called a couple of times a day, even a couple of times an hour. Thinking I could deal with even this, I "allowed" it. I had once had great success with another abrasive hospitalized patient by responding to his frequent demands to see me. He had gradually come to begin to develop some trust in my good will, becoming at the same time less demanding and abrasive.

Somehow Alicia did not react that way.

She only became more paranoid, repeating, "This isn't going to work. Nobody has wanted to talk to me since my Aunt Emily died."

Additionally, once I seemed to be accepting of her calling through the day, she escalated to calling throughout the night; getting no sufficiently strong negative reaction to nighttime calling, eventually she began to call at 2 and 3 a.m. Of course, she was testing me, and I was beginning to see her unique ability to find another person's limits. Mine appeared after two or three calls in the same night after 2:30 a.m.; I allowed my answering service to pick up the calls, thinking I would deal with her in our sessions. The other therapist had not had an unlisted home phone number and did not have an answering service connected to his phone. I did; this was going to be my solution.

I don't know whether I handled that well or badly. I called myself being "firm while gentle." I was beginning to understand why the previous therapist had behaved in what had appeared to be such a heartless manner.

Two things finally happened which drew our official professional relationship to a close. One was that Alicia became progressively more verbally threatening as she was unable to make her repeated telephone calls. (Not that she wasn't verbally abusive when she did reach me. After all, I "didn't care about her," and this "wasn't going to work.") She had begun to make threats about buying a gun and going down to the mental health center to shoot them all. I called her most recent therapist at that clinic and told her about these statements. There were some friends of mine working down there. Even without the laws about that kind of responsibility, I wanted them to be forewarned. I was concerned to learn that most of the staff did not take Alicia's threats seriously. I had the uneasy feeling she had the capacity to do just what she said she wanted to do.

While I was trying to figure out what to do next, I got a call from my answering service. They didn't want to take any more calls from this patient of mine; in fact, they seemed to be intimating they might discontinue my service if I didn't "do something" about this patient. At some point during that day, Alicia had called and told me she thought she might go down to my answering service building, spread gasoline on the carpet, and set their office on fire. I really was not eager to pass on that information to my already irate answering service. After all, the most violent act Alicia had ever actually performed was to throw the chairs around the office of the therapist who had referred her to me. She'd never been in jail. She'd never been hospitalized. Except for the time she had sat stubbornly in the mental health center waiting room, the police had never been called in regard to her.

I did tell them and I went out and bought a fire extinguisher.

I told Alicia my answering service had reached their tolerance level and I had reached mine for middle-of-the-night calls. Any more 2 a.m. calls and I'd have to stop seeing her. Oh no, she'd be good. She was sorry. She wanted to continue therapy.

Very soon thereafter, I got another 2 a.m. call (the second determining factor in our parting). Alicia knew she wasn't supposed to be calling that late but she felt suicidal. I said, "Then go down to the Emergency Room at Charity Hospital and admit yourself." She couldn't go to a hospital, she'd lose her apartment. If she went to the hospital and lost her apartment, could she come live with me? Deep inside me, some maternal element actually wanted to say yes. Some part of me heard the lost child that was way at the bottom of all the annoying behavior, the helplessness, the fear; and I also knew, my compassion notwithstanding, we weren't getting anywhere. I finally said, "Alicia, if you will go down to the Emergency Room and admit yourself, I'll continue to work with you. If you will not, we have to stop because I do not seem to know how to be effective with you. I want to be, but we both know it's not happening."

I never thought I'd terminate with a patient over the telephone, but I knew I was too intimidated to do it the right way. I just didn't want to take the risk. Better a bad live therapist than a good dead one.

That was, of course, not the last I heard of Alicia. There were subsequent calls which I didn't answer. I told my answering service she was no longer my patient. Although I realized my name was now surely on her list of those to be shot, the calls eventually tapered off. I know of two subsequent therapists after me and three others who had heard about her and wouldn't accept her in therapy. As long as 2 years afterward, I would suddenly get a call from her as she wore out yet another therapist, begging me to take her back. I would remind her each time that I had not been useful to her at the time and I could not in good conscience resume or continue therapy with somebody for whom I was not being therapeutic.

I have never felt very good about the outcome of my emotional sojourn with Alicia. The last I heard she had lost her nursing job, was washing dishes somewhere, and had generally deteriorated. I regret that I was not able to think of a way to contain her annoying behavior sufficiently to be able to work successfully with her. I think perhaps she might have become amenable to treatment with a year or so of hospitalization, but she had no money for private hospitalization; I very much doubt the local state hospital would have kept her more than their usual 3 months. After all, she wasn't clearly dangerous to herself and others, she was lucid, and she was functioning. I had the sense that her continued functioning was based on what she got through the peculiar acting-out behavior which was her substitute for therapy. I fantasied that when she finally ran through all the therapists in town, she would begin to disintegrate and would perhaps become more genuinely suicidal (or homicidal). She had refused to take medication. Perhaps it would have helped, but again, I didn't think so. It didn't much matter. Medication was under the heading of that about which she had chosen to be negativistic. I had been pushing for much more basic compromises, like her agreement to behave in such a way that I could stand her.

I wish there were some mechanism in our mental health world that would accommodate Alicia, some place she could be contained where there would be time and a context in which to give her the attention she needs.

Virginia Satir (1972) has delineated a set of behavioral stances which explain much of human behavior. In her observation of families through the years, she discovered four basic patterns that human beings begin, under stress, to employ. People always operate out of a need to maintain their self-esteem. When that self-esteem is threatened, a person will (1) blame the other party and discount the feelings of the other; (2) placate the other party and discount his or her own feelings; (3) become super-reasonable and discount both parties' feelings in favor of "the issues"; (4) behave irrelevantly, discounting reality and her or his whole context as well as anyone's feelings. I have found these concepts to be an invaluable guide through the years. Simply respecting another human being purposefully and, in some cases, doggedly, will go a long way in promoting the healing process. On more than one occasion I have been able to interrupt a psychotic "word salad" or recitation of delusional material simply by going toward the feeling I *guess* would be behind the apparently nonsensical sort of sentences.

Behind abrasiveness which serves to put off the would-be interactor, is, invariably, a desperate need for connection to another. The louder and harder the blaming, the greater the need. This energy can be redirected and used for constructive purposes as well as for destructiveness. Beneath the abrasiveness there is often a very delicate entity, generally in need of the quality of protection taking such an unpleasant form. I am thinking now of Eleanore. Eleanore is often quite abrupt in her manner, taking offense easily and responding sharply to slights which are barely perceptible to the other group members. She seems to be always close to boiling, prickly, and tight. Behind the fences and moats, she is a bona fide artist, a concert pianist. In therapy, Eleanore is learning to feel more solid in her ability to protect that delicate, sensitive self and is, therefore, softening; she is beginning to learn how to retain her blasts for occasions that truly warrant them. Eleanore can now listen long enough and well enough to be instructed about protecting her frightened infant self. She can also use her incisiveness on behalf of others, cutting through to the essence of an interaction and putting her group therapy on an honest track. That is the creative use of the components which come out abrasive when they are out of the individual's awareness.

I have a basic belief that there are not "untreatable" patients, but that there are therapists who do not know how to treat certain patients. I believe it is my responsibility to get the necessary supervision or training, or to refer the patient to the therapist who does have the appropriate skills. Alicia was a humbling experience for me. I did not find the key to inspire her to commit herself to therapy and to give up a significant amount of her demanding and unpleasant behavior. Additionally, I could not, in good conscience, send her to any colleague whose work I respected without telling the colleague what he or she would be getting into. If I *did* tell her or him, the chances of this person taking on Alicia were minimal. I finally decided I would *decrease* Alicia's odds of finding a therapist who could find a way to deal with her, by trying to refer her to somebody. The more the word got around town about her, the harder it would be for her to find anybody who would agree to her her (as has become the case).

Left to her own devices, maybe she would find some young therapist who didn't have enough experience to realize she was "impossible"; maybe there was some budding genius out there who had just graduated and who was still unknown to me. This tack didn't feel terribly responsible to me on my part. I was somewhat relieved that Alicia provided me with the opportunity to recommend that she hospitalize herself. I could, in good conscience, suggest that under the 3 a.m. circumstances. Since Alicia was also given to trying to find the therapist's home and banging on the door in the middle of the night, and since it was not impossible that *I* would end up having to call the police, I was glad I would at least be able to remind her that I'd made that recommendation.

Occasionally I wonder what my odds would have been had I been the first therapist instead of the fourth. Alicia was 36 by the time she got to me. Would it have worked at 26?

Alicia had a sister, her only living relative and, apparently, her only other social contact (besides the set of revolving, exasperated therapists). Would Ross Speck's and Carolyn Attneave's (1973) social network intervention therapy have broken this pattern? What if I had talked this desperate group of therapists into one giant convocation around Alicia? We were composed of two psychiatrists (one private, one state), three social workers (two private, one state), and one psychologist (private). Suppose we had all gathered with Alicia and perhaps the sister, for the sake of including all parts of her system. There would have been a question of whether to try to include her employer. Since she seemed to be managing on the job well enough to stay employed, I would have been hesitant to pull the one functional aspect of her life into the mass and vortex of the uncontrollable in which the rest of us seemed to be immersed with her. Additionally, I had a secret conviction that the nursing home where she was employed surely must not *know* the extent of her pathology. However, since she did subsequently lose the job, inclusion of the employer might have been indicated.

Whether we liked it or not, Alicia had put herself in the center of this group of therapists, bouncing around among them over a period of years. Even those who successfully maintained a physical distance from her were still included in her head as she talked with one of the others. I'm not sure how the question of fees for all involved could have been settled, but I suspect there was a point at which each one of us would have rather gladly *paid* just to be rid of the problem.

I was the rock and Alicia was the glacier. I still think she was moving; it was just too slow for any of us to calibrate. I think the dervish whirl of therapists she spun around herself had a protective function, albeit of an acting-out nature. Maybe it was *not* possible on an outpatient basis, but, had we been able to reach some creative and cooperative treatment plan, perhaps we could have found a way to turn the aggravation into something more useful. Maybe we all could have done something like assign each of ourselves a day to deal with Alicia and agree to be "on call" for one day a week, dividing the time into bits we could tolerate and going with the energy of her psychotic urgency until we found a way to quiet it in a humane, nonblaming way. Consciously and unresentfully allowing manipulation for a period of time can be useful in establishing sufficient trust in a demanding patient. This allowing can be a way of lifting the relationship out of the punitive framework the patient learned to expect from his/her family and subsequently creates around herself/himself in present day interactions.

That didn't happen with Alicia, but it did happen with Jerry, a bright and very obnoxious 18-year-old paranoid schizophrenic person who also manipulated his systems into becoming destructive entities. Jerry did not make it. He jumped off a downtown office building after manipulating the hospital into giving him a pass. I think Jerry *could* have made it, had we, who composed his family of therapists, been able to trust each other a little more. But he was much brighter than most of the staff in charge of him, and arrogant. I, who was in reality his primary therapist, was also much brighter than the rest of that staff and not sufficiently experienced or skilled to know how to make myself a nonthreatening person among the ancillary people. They didn't consider themselves ancillary, they considered *me* ancillary. They ran the wards and I was just a social worker. Not only that, I was a social worker on the adolescent service and Jerry had turned 19. He was out of my official milieu, automatically. Besides, the adult units felt the adolescent units coddled their patients and had "favored child" status with the administration. Were the psychiatrists and nurses going to listen to 27-year-old me, who had been out of school for a year and a half? Hardly. They grudgingly allowed me to visit Jerry on his new unit and questioned my motives for continuing to have that level of interest in him.

I was trying to save his *life*, that was all.

In the innocence of my youth, not yet understanding the entrenchment of schizophrenia, not knowing enough yet to know it "wasn't impossible" or would be "too draining," or whatever, I *had* reached Jerry before his transfer to the adult unit. The building structure was arranged in a series of "U's" and "L's". To go from my office to any other ward or office, I had to pass the half-door that was between the hall and the open unit for adolescent boys. My office was only a few doors from this half-door and within calling distance. Jerry would be hanging on the door whenever I passed, and would call out to me to come talk to him often when I wasn't passing. I would stop and give him a few minutes as I passed, without rebuking him for his demanding behavior. It seemed to me the rest of the staff provided more than enough rebuking. No doubt, they also provided the necessary limits that made my indulgences of him possible, but I had to wait until I had Alicia to teach me that important factor.

Part accident, part instinct, this arrangement and my sensitivity combined to work quite therapeutically for Jerry. Some of his abrasiveness began to subside and we developed a viable working relationship. He became more tolerable to the staff as the intensity of his demanding behavior abated. I think we would have made it and he would be alive today if he'd only been 17 instead of 18 and he hadn't been transferred to the adult unit and too far away from me. In 8 months, he made considerable improvement and was provisionally discharged. This event coincided with events in my own life which were of an almost mystical order (Brothers, 1976). In summary, I was suddenly and violently taken ill with a serious and life-threatening condition. Jerry somehow simultaneously became an orderly at the same hospital where I was admitted, and, without any of my doctors having any idea of what was going on, I did therapy with Jerry twice a day on his coffee breaks as I was quite literally hovering between life and death. I certainly planned none of that, but he showed up in my hospital room and it just seemed like the thing to do at the time. *Very* interestingly, Jerry improved dramatically, and his obnoxious behavior minimized to a point that nobody suspected he was my crazy patient.

After my discharge and during my convalescence, I did not see Jerry. He was in the care of a reasonably good mental health center who did arrange his readmission to the hospital when he seemed to be going downhill again. That is when he went to the adult unit. By then, I was back at work and could have continued with him had there been any way to bend the system to adequately accommodate that plan.

In Jerry's case, making myself extraordinarily available worked. In Alicia's case, I didn't find a way in. I don't know whether I had had too much personal therapy and experience to be able to do that kind of work again, or whether it is simply not possible to pursue it without the limits a hospital provides. "A wearing away" . . . the big question was what was going to be worn away. Would it be Alicia and Jerry's paranoid sheaths or would it be my patience and compassion? Would their heavily guarded, heavily damaged narcissism prevail and exclude all entry from the outside? Would it become a question of "me or you"? That was Jerry's issue with his mother. The thriving of one rhythmically affected the survival of the other. I managed to stand in for his mother for a little while in my own literal almost dying, giving Jerry time to get a toehold on life and living. But whatever malevolent forces exist in the phenomenon of paranoid schizophrenia beat us both. He could not hold out against the inner push to destruction without me. I could not make myself heard over my youth to heads of hospital units. Strange how his case feels more like a success to me than Alicia's, though she's alive and he is dead. Is that only my own narcissism? However fleetingly and infantile, he loved and trusted me for a little while. Did I simply find that more personally rewarding than the battle with Alicia? Had he covered his vulnerability with the amount of rage Alicia employed, would he still be alive? Does it count anywhere in the cosmos that I still think of him fondly?

This paper feels incomplete to me; I don't know how to end it. The two processes of Jerry and me, then Alicia and me, didn't complete. Jerry abruptly terminated his end of what was going on between us. I'm still working on my end. That became obvious to me as I find myself writing about him with tears still welling up, though it has been nearly 16 years now. I terminated my end with Alicia, reluctantly on the one hand and with great relief on the other. Yet, I still wonder if there were a way, which I just didn't discover, that would have led to her center and to her eventual healing.

REFERENCES

Brothers, B. J. (1976). The power of my weakness. In S. Kopp (Ed.), *The naked therapist* (pp. 181–188). San Diego, CA: EDITS.

Funk & Wagnalls. (1978). *New comprehensive international dictionary of the English language.* New York: The Publishers Guild Press.

Satir, V. (1972). *Peoplemaking.* Palo Alto, CA: Science and Behavior Books.

Speck, V., & Attneave, C. L. (1973). *Family networks.* New York: Pantheon Books.

ing and was presumably acting in an industrial engineering capacity. His uniformly poor performance on all tests of intellectual functioning was considered sufficient validation for the decision to remove him. There was no mention in my report of his having an abrasive personality and the validity of the test findings was questioned because of his apparent fearfulness.

This story has a complex ending. The man stayed with the multi-national corporation. He got a headquarters staff job involved with overseeing industrial engineering functions for that particular continent. Apparently the people in power within that country inside the organization were able to get rid of him locally but he was not without influence among the executives who were responsible for operations on that continent. There had been a power struggle. The local faction had won a temporary victory by having him removed. But they were outflanked by another group with power in the organization.

Some years later I was present when a senior executive responsible for corporate staff functions relating to that continent confronted the psychologist then directing the company's assessment center. He alleged that a hatchet job had been carried out on the employee and accused the assessment center of participating. In his opinion, the employee had been doing an excellent job for several years in his headquarters assignment.

Fortunately, the integrity of my report spoke for itself. I reported the poor test findings as well as the fact that the person seemed disturbed by the immediate situation he was in. I did not endorse any of the rumors that had been passed along to me about his abrasive personality.

When confronted by these facts, the psychologist then in charge of the assessment center offered the executive who initiated the confrontation the opportunity to have this man retested. Perhaps the low test scores had indeed been a product of situational anxiety. The offer was declined.

As the story illustrates, labeling people abrasive personalities can have significant consequences. It can also backfire.

I have not found the concept abrasive person useful or comforting. Yet I suspect that other people have used the label with respect to me. Perhaps it is a relative concept. Who abrades whom? Or in terms of the physical metaphor, which material abrades which—diamond dust will cut a hard steel, metal filings will make a shambles of plastics, teeth or claws will tear flesh.

A surprise attack can certainly inflict pain and damage. But how can one person *continually* irritate another? Why does the abraded one remain vulnerable to the actions of the abrader? Is the latter an all-powerful torturer or prison guard? Does s/he conditionally give valuable goods that entice people to endure suffering from his or her acts? Is s/he so creative that his or her actions are a continual surprise and no adaptive response is possible? I suspect that when someone persists in being irritating and people persist in staying in that person's company at least some of the above conditions must be met.

There are undoubtedly voice tones which convey a strong biological or culturally conditioned message. The whine of complaint, the cry of distress, the threat implicit in anger—perhaps abrasive people use these tonalities when others think they are not called for. If we hear tonalities expressing distress from our patients, however, we probably should not be surprised. Perhaps they are effective communicators rather than abrasive people.

The longer I am in practice the more tolerant I find I have become of patient's communicative styles. I now no longer find a patient's communicative style irritating or offensive when I have the option to be curious or to find it interesting instead. After all the patient is paying for my attention and my time. I have to learn to adapt to the person's communicative style in order to establish a relationship. If this style causes me distress, then perhaps I'm not really competent to work with that person. Another possibility is that this is an opportunity for me to learn how to respond more flexibly.

In group settings, disruptive behavior can be a problem. But this too can be a challenge to group cohesion and group flexibility. The best example I have of the challenge that an abrasive person can present is a patient who insisted on being treated in a group.

Sylvia, a sturdy woman in her 40s, was referred by a referral service of one of the professional groups of which I am a member. She had been in various kinds of therapy for over 15 years. While she believed that therapy had been a valuable experience for her, the truth of this conclusion might not have been apparent to an unbiased observer. She worked sporadically at temporary clerical jobs. Partly as a result of therapy, she had separated from her family and had only a limited relationship with her children. She was chronically short of money. She wanted an apartment of her own but could only afford furnished residence accommodations of various kinds.

Her relationships with men were problematic. Occasionally she took money from them but this had become a relatively rare supplement to her income. She also got occasional sums from her parents. She really wanted a man who would be willing to support her without expecting too much in return.

She wanted to be in a group. She had recently been asked to leave two different group-therapy settings because her behavior was not acceptable to the group leaders. She had been in two groups with her last therapist and had achieved a dominant position in these groups which she found gratifying. The therapist had died and the groups had disbanded. Apparently it was this experience that she was seeking to replace.

I told her that my groups were relatively structured and oriented to people working on achieving specific outcomes in their everyday lives.* Though she had many potential projects for making changes in her life, she did not seem committed to taking responsibility for making anything specific happen. I said that unless she committed herself to specific change projects she was not likely to benefit from the group, but that I thought she could be a useful challenge to other group members.

I offered to refer her to other group-therapy contexts where self-expression, the formation of relationships, or the interpretation of behavior were more central, since these seemed to be aspects of group therapy that were more familiar to her. I also offered to work with her on an individual basis since only in such a setting could she have virtually all of the therapeutic attention to herself. She wanted to work with me but only in a group setting. She agreed to come to six sessions of one of my clinical groups to see if this would be beneficial for her. She continued coming to this group for several months, usually paying for the opportunity. She did not report any benefits nor were there any significant changes in her life that an unbiased observer could be likely to regard as beneficial.

This woman was consistently unpleasant in many gross and subtle ways. Her voice was loud and harsh much of the time. She frequently did not look at people when speaking to them. She usually spoke about people in the third person rather than addressing them directly. She frequently looked at her hands as she picked at her nails while speaking. She had no difficulty, however, looking directly at people to express anger, contempt, or hostility and did so on numerous occasions.

Many of her exchanges were interruptions. Her typical communications were complaints, edgy questions, and uninvited interpretations or criticisms. She arrived for sessions late, tried to take up a larger share of the group's time than she was entitled to, and consistently failed to cooperate with requests or suggestions.

For group members she became a challenge. They tried in various ways to be nice to her and to win her over to a more positive mode of relating. She did not reciprocate. They were generally supportive of her criticisms and complaints against me. If only I had left the group Sylvia might have been satisfied to stay indefinitely. I, however, continued to interrupt her interruptions and to give priority to working on projects where people stated definite outcomes they were willing to work toward. Sylvia stormed out of the group in midsession several times and missed sessions sporadically. She continued to explore other group experiences but they did not satisfy her or she was not permitted to stay. When she finally walked out permanently, she had arranged for alternative treatment.

---

*For a description of such a skill-learning, problem-solving group see: Greenberg, George, with Zeigler, Deborah J. "Getting Fired: Crisis and Opportunity in Midlife," VOICES: The Art and Science of Psychotherapy, (1982), *18*(1), 66-73.

I heard from her by phone nearly a year later. There had been no significant change in her circumstances, but she was continuing in another therapy group. We had provided her with a transitional experience in being connected to other people but with no opportunity or incentive to really modify her behavior. Group members learned from her example how inflexible people can insist on being and that they could cope with her style and continue to pursue their own objectives. Sylvia made the problem people in their lives seem easy by comparison.

Despite her best efforts Sylvia abraded nobody in any permanent way. People occasionally responded with anger to her provocations, but usually they relied on me to halt her interruptions. In general, she was treated with care, respect, and consideration. By the time she left, however, everyone in the group agreed that they really did not like having her around.

I don't think that Sylvia was psychotic though she probably would be diagnosed as a borderline personality. She seemed unwilling to care about anything except her own feelings and impulses. While she valued her experiences in psychotherapy, they probably contributed to the abrasive pattern of her behavior. She had held a full time job, married, and become the mother of several children before she began therapy. It was her experience of bioenergetically oriented therapy and the rhetoric of the woman's movement that led her to throw off the burdens of husband, children, and regular employment. Despite the freedom of action and expression she insisted on, she was generally lonely, isolated, and depressed. She could seduce people into becoming engaged with her but did not offer most people enough to stay involved.

She really wanted someone, preferably a man, to come along and take care of her, to provide her with money, set her up in an apartment, and allow her to take charge of the relationship. She was inordinately confident about the validity and appropriateness of her opinions, judgments, and impulses. Probably she had internalized models who behaved with such aggressive confidence but had enough power, skill, or other resources to maintain more adequate social relationships.

As an extreme case, Sylvia exemplifies most features people consider abrasive. She was consistently irritating in her manner. While she kept wanting someone with power and authority to help her, she refused to act in a fashion that respected the rights and importance of others in relation to her. She would shout and interrupt, but at no time did she become physically violent or abusive. Ultimately she always respected people's right to ask her to leave their premises. Probably she realized that if she crossed the boundary into physically abusing people or flagrantly trespassing on their property rights, she might lose some of her freedom to act as she wished. Also despite her disregard of others, she was still capable of feeling embarrassed by a sense of social disapproval or personal failure.

Ultimately, she could control her abrasive behavior sufficiently so that most people would only abandon her and not engage in serious reprisals. When people cross the boundary into physically injuring people or property, others stop considering them abrasive and begin regarding them as dangerous or criminal. Eventually serious reprisals and injuries are likely to ensue. The therapist should, for everyone's safety and protection, be able to assess accurately the person's ability to keep unpleasant behavior from turning into seriously damaging behavior.

People's abrasiveness is likely to be a greater problem when they have more power than Sylvia does. When people feel that they must remain engaged with someone because of consideration of employment or family bonding, then behavior like Sylvia's, if maintained over a period of time, may become seriously detrimental to the well-being of others. Unless they can sufficiently insulate themselves from abrasive behavior people may develop stress symptoms and become hostile themselves. If they can't express hostility to the abrasive person they may direct it toward weaker associates.

When people complain about other people's abrasiveness, it may be important to examine their own motives rather than to join the project of evaluating and/or changing someone else's behavior. In the case of the abrasive executive it was clear that this was part of a power play somehow to discredit him. In the case of Sylvia, group members learned that they did not have to change her in order to get on with their own projects. It was Sylvia who spent most of her time and energy complaining about the inadequacies of other people and hoping that this would somehow result in a change in her own status or their behavior. If we stay in contact with abrasive people perhaps they are offering us something that we can really make good use of.

Abrasion:
Wearing Down and Transformation

Donald D. Lathrop

I have significant resistance to writing an article about the abrasive *patient* (and not the abrasive therapist) for a journal devoted to therapists talking about patients instead of themselves. Only my trust in Mark Stern and Jerry Travers permits me to write this. I know them both to be fully aware of the dangers of unexamined countertransferences in both the conduct of and writing about psychotherapy.

Abrasion is relative; abrasion is subjective. For the "virgin" diamond, uncut, unpolished, abrasion is the indispensable process in the revelation of both its inner beauty and its potential usefulness. This is equally true for the psyche and it matters not whether that is the psyche of the patient or of the therapist. Like the diamond, abrasion alone is not sufficient to produce the uniqueness we call individuation in the psyche. Knowledge of crystalline structure (psychodynamics), experience in working with material of every possible quality, skill in striking exactly the right blow at the right moment in the right place are essential in both transformations. The abrasive patient, like the irregular diamond, is essential for the education of the true artisan.

Whether in gem cutting or in psychotherapy, one learns only by doing. "Mistakes" are absolutely inevitable and are indispensable for the development of anything other than a mere technician. (Most psychotherapists, all counselors, are mere "technicians"; probably this is true of gem cutters—and all other categories of human endeavor—as well.) The fundamental element in learning that makes "growth" out of a "mistake" is staying involved and cleaning up one's mess. In psychotherapy, that means resisting (or recovering from) the inevitable impulse to blame the other person for the mistake. With the abrasive, abusive patient, this impulse is often irresistible and can only be restrained by competent supervision. In the "old days," and still in the highly structured training programs for therapists, supervision was/is understood as a natural part of one's development as a therapist, in the same way that being a patient in

Donald D. Lathrop, M.D., graduated from Tufts University Medical School in 1954. He is presently in private practice and co-director of The Relationship Center in Boise, as well as having institutional affiliations.

therapy was/is. With the rush of ego psychologies of the past 20 years (Perls' Gestalt, Berne's Transactional Analysis), with the dominance of California consciousness and values on the whole society, personal experience as a patient and extended and varied experiences in supervision are unknown to the vast majority of mental health providers. Techniques and gimmicks have taken the place of in-depth knowledge and experience of the psyche (the unconscious, Freud's id, our instinctual side, our animal side).

A mistake in a relationship is any event which threatens to destroy the creative potential of that relationship. All mistakes in psychotherapy are the result of incomplete understanding on the part of the therapist of what the patient is thinking or feeling. Usually, this is accompanied by projection by the therapist onto the patient of some unwanted, negative aspect of himself/herself. In ordinary psychotherapy terminology, a mistake is an incorrect, incorrectly timed, inappropriate intervention, including interpretation. Being insensitive to the other person, reading the other person incorrectly, imposing one's own stuff on the other person without acknowledging that one is doing that, are all part of mistakes in psychotherapy. Just as the gem cutter recognizes a mistake immediately by the shattering of the rough stone, the sensitive and alert psychotherapist notes the fragmentation of the patient's ego, however brief, however slight, however carefully concealed. Where the masters in psychotherapy learned this phenomenon was in the psychotherapy of schizophrenics. Since the psychotherapy of schizophrenia is now largely passé and not a part of the contemporary training programs for psychotherapists, today's therapy initiates must learn this by the treatment of borderline personalities. Although analytic training programs still explore these depth processes, the identification of such blunders is dependent upon the knowledge and ability of the trainers. No teacher of psychotherapy is as skilled and effective as the schizophrenic patient in confronting the therapist with the fact of having made a mistake. Furthermore, the opportunity to have this experience, to make these mistakes with hospitalized patients (who are less likely to commit suicide as a signal that a mistake has been made) is almost nonexistent today. In addition, the ever-present threat of lawsuits make today's therapists appropriately fearful of making mistakes, thus unwilling to take the risks that are inherent in the process of depth psychotherapy. All of these factors make it increasingly improbable that new psychotherapists will learn depth psychotherapy or that abusive, abrasive patients will receive corrective treatment.

Committing a mistake in psychotherapy is not a "sin," and need not be destructive to the therapy, provided the therapist is able to acknowledge the mistake and to stay with the patient through all of the consequences of the mistake. If the patient commits suicide, this means staying with the survivors until they have worked through their grief and rage sufficiently to get on with their lives. In the less drastic mistakes that all of us make day in and day out (from fatigue, from insensitivity, from burnout, from the intrusion of our own problems into our work), being aware of the mistake and acknowledging it to *oneself* is the essential first step. Sometimes it is necessary to acknowledge the mistake to the patient, but this should never be used as a manipulation by the therapist to gain forgiveness from the patient for having made the mistake in the first place. There is no valid general rule about self-revelation by the therapist in psychotherapy. Therapists' personalities differ markedly in this respect. The issue is not whether one should acknowledge the mistake to the patient; the issue is being able to acknowledge the mistake to oneself.

The abrasive patient, by definition, seizes upon the mistake as a wonderful opportunity to berate the therapist. This is one of those exquisitely delicate points in an intimate relationship. If the patient succeeds in "killing off" the therapist, the healing value of the relationship is destroyed. If the therapist fails to accept full responsibility for the mistake or permits the patient to beat him/her up, maladaptive patterns will be perpetuated in both personalities. In Jung's (1972) analysis of the interaction between God and Job, Job finally figures out that God has made a terrible, stupid mistake. God never cops to this, but Job is released from his own endless torment by the breaking of his parental transference regarding God's omniscience and benevolence.

What we learn from our mistakes in psychotherapy is more about psychodynamics—the natural laws that describe the movement of forces in the psyche. We do not learn the "right way" to be either therapists or human beings. The implication of the Judeo-Christian ethic, of psychoanalytic theory, that there is a right way to be, is a cruel hoax. Only consciousness can free us from that timeless expectation. What kind of deity would not say, "I am *the* Way, *the* Truth, *the* Light?" Still, the skilled psychotherapist teaches the patient to discover his/her own way, not to become a clone of the therapist or of the prevailing deity.

It is in the area of character analysis that the ego-psychology technicians are especially inept. Even the body therapies (which have grown out of Reich's pioneering work) have been largely superficial and limited to psychic material accessible to ego consciousness. The typically American "10-session cure" of Ida Rolf is a good example. The most widely experienced of all contemporary psychotherapies, EST, is nothing more than a psychological face-lift, with results as transient as the "training" itself.

Depth psychotherapy—the exquisitely delicate exploration of the psyche by techniques that intensify the relationship and maintain the focus on the patient's inner life—still lives. Only a tiny percentage of today's therapists/counselors (or their prospective patients/clients) seek depth therapy, either for themselves or as a tool for clinical work. For those who do, the abrasive patient offers the diligent self-exploring therapist an unequaled opportunity. Through such work, we may achieve consciousness of our own character structure and character traits. These are the architectural framework of the personality. Like the foundation and frame of a building, these elements are concealed from conscious view in the completed structure.

I want to illustrate the difficulty of this task, the resistances the ego has to acknowledging powerful structural elements in the psyche over which it can never have control.

As a trainee, I felt contempt for most of my teachers. One particularly slippery professor urged me to stick with the patients I hated, the ones I wanted to dump, the ones I was positive could not benefit from anything I had to offer. In many instances, my perceptions were correct. The reality, however, was that I was there to learn, not to "cure" people.

This admonition to continue to struggle with the obviously impossible, untreatable, unrewarding patients stirred rageful memories of my mother. I remembered the countless times when she would complete her, "You'll be the death of me" statement with the clincher: "Someday, when you have children of your own, you'll understand the misery you are putting me through. Then it will be your turn to suffer the selfishness, the ingratitude you show me." Of course she was right. The professor was right. It is my own narcissistic wound I have been trying to escape. What I have tried to do differently than my mother, perhaps my teachers, is to not lay an additional burden of guilt on my children/patients for "making me go through the pain" of raising them, teaching them, sticking with them through whatever they needed to experience in order to grow up.

The abrasive patient is a personality, a specific character ("crystalline") structure that abrades a facet of the therapist's own character structure that is unpolished, unexposed to light of consciousness. The therapeutic relationship is no different in this regard than any other relationship. We all know people we don't like, people with whom we have horrendous conflicts. Most of us know these people have certain qualities that exist in us and that we do not wish to "own." Those of us who have been through a divorce know that all of us, at times, choose to remove ourselves from the relationship with the abrasive-other-person. It is a relic of Freud's early theorizing (as well as a cornerstone of the ego psychologies) to believe that we can "work it out," "make the unconscious conscious." It remained for Jung to show us that the "unconscious" is limitless, that it can never be "emptied out," that there is no one way or right way to be a whole human being. It is a matter of common experience that we can only go as far in a relationship as the potential and commitment of the individuals involved permits.

Why, then, not simply "divorce" the abrasive patient? Aside from all of the wonderful, high-level, "spiritual" reasons for staying in such a pain-producing relationship, there are a couple of other dimensions relevant to psychotherapy. One is economic. Certainly for the private practitioner, often for the institutional therapist, it is simply economically impossible to get rid of all of the personality types one experiences as abrasive.

The other variable that is particularly important to my own mentality is that psychotherapy is a well-structured relationship in which I feel in more control than in other kinds of relationships. The other person, the patient, is giving me implied consent to impose my values, perceptions, beliefs upon him/her in hopes of effecting changes in his/her consciousness, personality, experience of life. Universally, the patient is seeking relief from some kind of pain, whether from within or imposed by external persons who have some power over him/her (parents, spouses, lovers, police, judges, employers, and so forth). One tiny, but not insignificant, dimension to this special relationship called psychotherapy is that I know that each encounter, however painful for me, is finite. The hour will come to an end. The interview will be over. The other person will go back to where they live (whether a psychiatric ward, their home, or an institution) and I will go to my mine. In marriage, love affairs, business relationships, social encounters, I have no such control, no such assurance. I may, indeed, feel trapped in the relationship forever. (Again, those who have been through divorce, especially more than once, will recognize this feeling readily.)

Although I have been a Jungian for more than 20 years, it was not until I read Lyn Cowan's (1982) book, *Masochism, a Jungian View*, in 1983 that I accepted my own deliberate exposure to suffering as nonpathological. While I have successfully treated the most abrasive imaginable personalities, while I have learned and relearned the lessons enumerated in this article, I have always regarded my pain as a demonstration of my own sickness. The Judeo-Christian ethic that suffering and redemption are related has always added to the burden of the pain intrinsic to abrasion. The image of Christ on the cross, of my mother's, my own, or the patient's martyrdom, has always been and continues to be revulsive to me. I don't want you to hear me as saying, "Stay with the abrasive patient; the experience—however painful—will help you grow, will make you a better person, a better therapist." Mere suffering produces no transformation. Without some direction from the ego as to the meaning of the pain it is experiencing, nothing is gained, no one benefited.

The patients who are most abrasive to me are: (a) women who hate men, whose fathers abused, rejected, or abandoned them; (b) men or women who are totally identified with the mother aspect of the psyche, especially those who righteously believe they are "good" mothers; (c) men and women in the manic phase of manic-depressive illness; (d) men and women with rigid, feelingless, obsessive-compulsive personalities;

and (e) people who have contempt for and are hostile to the feminine aspect of consciousness. I'm specifically talking about abrasive, not just difficult, complicated, demanding, troublesome people. For example, alcoholic and other addicted personalities may be very difficult for me, but I do not find them abrasive unless they specifically include the characteristics in the above list.

Abrasive patients, like all other kinds of patients, rarely come to therapy for complete reconstruction of their lives. Most courses of psychotherapy, whether with the abrasive or with the lovable patient, are relatively brief, relatively problem oriented, relatively uninvolving. It is with the occasional individuals who are committed to whatever is required in order to make major, permanent changes in themselves that abrasive personality qualities require the highest degree of skill, the greatest self-discipline of which the therapist is capable.

My "favorite" abusive patient was a woman who despised men, who abused me regularly with her perceptive, accurate attacks on my vulnerable fear of dependency on women, who tolerated my occasional outbursts of verbal abuse of her for her unrelenting hostility toward men, who quit therapy one time less than I kicked her out, who went to a number of other therapists for necessary support during the time she was in treatment with me, who although she was a highly successful business woman involved herself in a training program for volunteer lay therapists, who stayed with me, as I stayed with her, through the entire process.

One of the little, side issues in our relationship was that she insisted repeatedly that I should have sex with her. Since she was a very sexual woman, since she couldn't find any men who would have or were capable of having sex with her, since we talked about sex a lot, since it was clear that I enjoy and appreciate sexual relating, since she was wealthy enough, powerful enough, successful enough to hire men to do anything that she wanted them to do, it made sense that I should provide that service as part of my employment by her. A careful reading of both Freud and Jung reveals that both men developed their theories to protect themselves from fucking attractive, available, vulnerable female patients. Indeed, it was my cognitive beliefs about the correct conduct of psychotherapy that enabled me to resist this insistent and highly attractive invitation. It is, in fact, the therapist's rejection of the sexual seduction without rejecting the whole person that constitutes the core of successful resolution of "transference neurosis," the healing of the incest wound from which we all suffer at the level of soul.

Following the successful completion of our 3-year therapeutic relationship, that middle-aged woman went on to make a successful marriage with an appropriate man from her "real" life. Somewhat later, as a result of my own continued efforts in my own behalf, I, too, was able to remarry. That woman did not cure me, nor I her. It was our faithful adherence to the well-known healing process of depth psychotherapy that led each of us to the transformation we sought.

Patients are ultimately our principal teachers. The abrasive patient who is willing to endure the process of transformation is the most potent teacher about our character structure.

REFERENCES

Cowan, L. (1982). *Masochism, a Jungian view*. Dallas, TX: Spring Publications.
Jung, C. G. (1972). *The answer to Job*. Princeton, NJ: Princeton University Press.

The Care and Feeding of Abrasiveness

Alvin R. Mahrer

I want to answer three questions about abrasiveness in patients, and I want to answer from the perspective of experiential psychotherapy: (a) What is the meaning of abrasiveness? What is it that can be referred to and defined as abrasiveness? (b) What does the therapist do with that abrasiveness? (c) What happens to the abrasiveness over the course of psychotherapy?

THE EXPERIENTIAL MEANING OF ABRASIVENESS

If we are going to talk seriously about abrasiveness, we had better specify what we mean by that term. I suspect it is somewhat illusory to pretend that there is mutual agreement, and then for each perspective to rush off with a glaringly different meaning when we get down to actual therapeutic work.

It Is Something the Therapist Feels and Experiences

Our abrasiveness occurs when most of the therapist's attention is on whatever most of the patient's attention is on, and when the therapist is mainly being in the same scene or situational context that the patient is being in. Accordingly, both patient and therapist may be sitting in the living room with the rather wimpish visitor, and both patient and therapist are attending to the somewhat inane remarks of the visitor. Or, both the patient and therapist are at the department store, attending predominantly to the smooth pressure from the refrigerator salesman. Both patient and therapist are living in some scene, some situational context, some state, and most of their attention is directed onto something—the external remark, look, gesture, or internal thoughts, feelings, bodily state.

Alvin R. Mahrer, Ph.D., who completed his doctoral studies in 1954 at the University of Ottawa, is Professor in the Faculty of Psychology of the University of Ottawa. He was formerly on the faculties of the University of Waterloo (Ontario) and Miami University (Ohio).

I want to express my appreciation to Lise Abhukara for her assistance in the preparation of this article.

Under these conditions, abrasiveness is something in and of me. It is my abrasiveness. I feel it in me. It is the experiencing of abrasiveness here in me. It is alive and occurring right now. If someone were to ask where it is, I would point to me, to my way of being, to feelings and experiencings in me.

It is not something the therapist sees in the patient, while the therapist feels and experiences something else. We must draw a careful distinction between the above meaning of abrasiveness as contrasted with the more common meaning in which it is something the therapist sees in the patient. In most approaches, the therapist attends predominantly to the patient, and the therapist sees it in the patient, notices signs of it in the patient, clinically infers it, observes it, responds, and reacts to it—and it is uniformly identified by the external therapist as occurring over there in the patient.

It is the external therapist, attending mainly to the patient, who labels it as abrasiveness, who defines it, organizes it, constructs it by means of seeing and observing it over there in the patient. In so doing, the therapist is not feeling or experiencing abrasiveness. Instead, the therapist may be in the role of the astute clinical observer, may be feeling some fear or annoyance at the patient whom the therapist then calls abrasive, may be having all sorts of feelings and experiencings about the patient's abrasiveness. When the therapist stands off and sees it in the patient, and when the therapist feels and experiences something other than abrasiveness, we are talking about a common meaning of abrasiveness, but not the experiential meaning.

It Is a Characteristic Way of Being and Experiencing in the Session

It is a continuing characteristic rather than a singular achievement. In our meaning, abrasiveness refers to something which occurs fairly frequently throughout the session and across sessions. It is a sustained way of being and experiencing. If the patient is assaultive or threatening or abusive, this occurs rather frequently, even characteristically. I am excluding abrasiveness which occurs so rarely that its appearance almost constitutes a singular achievement by the patient.

It is surface, operational, expressed, rather than deeper, internal, intrapsychic. Our meaning of abrasiveness focuses on something which is right here on the surface. One is being-doing-feeling-expressing abrasiveness. It is not something which is deeper in personality, not a deeper process or potential. In experiential therapy, abrasiveness may either be located on the operating surface or at a deeper level, but the abrasiveness we are talking about here is that which occurs on the surface, that which is expressed and shown. It is present, expressed, threatening, reviling, damaging.

It may be related to any kind of deeper potential or internal personality process. If the abrasiveness we are describing is on the surface, shown, expressed, the theory of experiential psychotherapy holds that virtually anything may be deeper. The more you grasp whatever is occurring at a deeper level, the more you grasp the specific nature of what underlies the surface abrasiveness in this person right now, the more you are appreciating something singular and distinctive in this particular person. Underlying this momentary abrasiveness may be a deeper experiencing of equalizing my status and my worth with you, or it may consist of the awful deeper experiencing of being below you, less than you, of no worth at all. The deeper experiencing may consist of my being hated and unwanted by you. It may be the bad experiencing of having no presence, without substance, of having no impact or effect upon you, of being a vacuum of nothingness. It may consist of the deeper experiencing of reaching, you, rubbing up against you, closing the gap between us, being up against you. It may be the experiencing of soft gentleness, sensuous caressing, languorous touching. Or it may be the deeper experiencing of explosive violence, monstrous assaultiveness, uncontrolled fury, unrelenting damage-inflection.

It includes an external agent. Some ways of being and experiencing can occur when I am alone. Without another person directly participating, I can manage to be and feel scared or depressed or confused or separated. But I really need a companion or target in order to rub someone the wrong way, to assault, to toss my violence at, to shower with abrasiveness. In experiential therapy, this companion or target is someone upon whom the patient's attention is centered: the enemy, victim, co-worker, sibling, most anyone. In many therapies, the therapist fulfills the role of the targeted external agent.

It is not something which is referred to or talked about. Our meaning of abrasiveness included a way of being or experiencing which is surface, operating, expressed. The patient is being and experiencing it, and it is shared by the being and experiencing therapist. Abrasiveness, in experiential psychotherapy, is not something which the patient talks about while neither being nor experiencing it. A patient may refer to acts of verbal abuse, may tell about threatening violence toward someone, may recite stories of his or her abrasiveness, relate its history, explain its likely psychological causes, talk about his or her reactions to it. But if it is referred to and talked about, and if it is not right here and now in the person's behavior, being, feeling, and experiencing, it is outside the experiential meaning of abrasiveness. It is being and experiencing one way while referring to or talking about something called abrasiveness.

THE THERAPEUTIC USE OF ABRASIVENESS

Therapeutic work begins in each session when the patient gets settled in the chair, has eyes closed, deploys most of his or her attention onto some meaningful center, and allows at least moderate bodily sensations to occur. There is minimal attending to the therapist, minimal talking to or interaction with the therapist in this beginning of therapeutic work. Under these conditions, the being and experiencing of abrasiveness is grist for the therapeutic mill. But what about the patient whose abrasiveness is leveled directly at the therapist before therapeutic work begins?

Abrasiveness Directed Toward the Therapist

Typically we are considering the first few sessions prior to the time when the patient enters into therapeutic work. Under these conditions there are at least three guidelines.

1. *Before the therapeutic work starts, this is just a relationship co-constructed by therapist and patient.* Before both therapist and patient get into the posture of starting therapeutic work, they are two persons merely interacting and interrelating with one another. This may last a few minutes or longer. Whatever kind of interactive relationship occurs is a conjoint, co-constructed product of the two persons. Ordinarily this lasts only a few minutes, and they start therapeutic work. If, however, therapist and patient interrelate so as to bring about an abrasive patient whose abusiveness is targeted directly onto the therapist, then that is the kind of relationship the two have succeeded in co-constructing with one another. Here is abrasiveness, coming from the patient and directed toward the therapist. What does the therapist do?

2. *The therapist invites the patient to begin therapeutic work.* The invitation is to get the body settled, close the eyes, let the attention go to a meaningful center (not the therapist), and allow bodily sensations to occur. Most of the time, the patient will go into an experiential state in which the abrasiveness heightens, and is targeted toward some key figure or situational context. The menacing or the antagonism or the abusiveness pours onto the more meaningful figure in the more meaningful situation. Often the patient will start therapeutic work by entering into some other experiential state, no longer being or experiencing the abrasiveness. Leaving behind the abrasiveness for something more meaningful illuminates the abrasiveness as a co-constructed product of the patient-therapist team rather than an intrinsic characteristic of the patient. In either condition, the abrasiveness becomes grist for the therapeutic mill, or it is set aside in favor of more important therapeutic work.

3. *If the patient chooses to direct abrasiveness toward the therapist,
therapeutic work does not begin.* It is the therapist's responsibility to in-
vite the patient to begin therapeutic work. It is the patient's right, responsibility, and choice either to begin or not to begin. Almost always, the
abrasive-acting patient elects to begin therapeutic work, and it is no
longer directed toward the therapist. However, sometimes the patient
continues to direct the abrasiveness toward the therapist. The patient
keeps on menacing the therapist, chiding the therapist, threatening the
therapist, abusing the therapist, or whatever. Under this condition, therapeutic work cannot and does not begin. We may begin a few minutes
later, much later, or not at all. We may try another session. We may
never begin therapeutic work. The choice is predominantly in the hands
of the patient.

The Therapist's Locus and the Nature of Therapeutic Data

Once therapeutic work begins, the therapist may be in the locus of the
teacher or instructor. In this position, the therapist is external to the patient, showing the patient what to do next, explaining how to do it, giving
free choice on whether or not to take the next step in the session. Otherwise, the therapist is alongside or with the patient, sharing the patient's
attentional center and experiential state, being and feeling and experiencing along with the patient (Mahrer, 1983).

In this locus, there are two interrelated kinds of therapeutic data. One
consists of some kind of scene or situational context in which both patient
and therapist are being and existing. The second consists of the experiencing which is occurring in the therapist who is joined or fused or along
with the patient. This may well consist of the abrasiveness, or it may consist of a deeper experiencing underlying the abrasiveness. Accordingly,
the therapeutic data may consist of being and existing in a scene with the
patient's childhood acquaintances, and the experiencing may be that of
menacing or abusing the neighborhood pansy, or it may be that of experiencing a deeper sense of being a nothing, a nonentity, a vacuum. The
therapeutic data, then, consist of some scene or situation, constructed by
the patient's immediate statements and behaviors, and some kind of experiencing. In all of this, the therapist is along with the patient, joined
with the patient in being in some scene and undergoing some experiencing.

*Versus the external locus in which the therapist "does something about
the patient's abrasiveness."* Many other therapies construct a qualitatively different topography in which the therapist is external to the patient, the therapist sees abrasiveness pouring out of the patient, and the
therapist who is the target must do something about the patient's abra-

siveness. Here is a constructed opposition in which patient and therapist are up against one another. The therapist paints the abrasiveness as bad, as a block to therapeutic progress, as resistance of interference, as downright personally insulting or menacing or dangerous. Nose against nose, force against force, therapists search for effective weapons in their efforts to "do something about the patient's abrasiveness."

Therapists turn to one another to find effective specialized methods and tactics such as interpreting the abrasiveness as resistance, getting around the abrasiveness, trying to overcome the abrasiveness, trying to discourage it or set "appropriate" limits on it, trying to get the underlying psychodynamics, trying to "work it through," trying to motivate the patient to give up the abrasiveness, trying to defuse it, trying to work with the therapist's galloping reactions to the patient's abrasiveness, trying to stand up against it valiantly (Chrzanowski, 1977, 1978, 1980; Fromm, 1981; Michels, 1977; Rosen, 1955; Saretsky, 1981; West, 1978).

Versus regarding it as a problem/symptom to be "treated". Faced with the patient's challenging and menacing abrasiveness, caught in the oppositional arena of the relationship, the locus of many non-experiential therapists is one-on-one opposition, and the therapeutic data feature the attacking abrasiveness exploding from the patient. Accordingly, it is understandable that the patient's abrasiveness be regarded as something bad, sick, maladjustive, pathological, problematic, symptomatic, neurotic, or psychotic, or diagnostic. It is understandable that it must be treated: reduced, cured, extinguished, modified, taken in hand, taught a lesson, controlled, trephined.

Once it is regarded as a problem/symptom to be treated, it is easy to search for the commonalities in such abusive, difficult, menacing, acting-out, abrasive patients. We search and find commonalities in personality traits, early history, precipitating causes, character, mental status, psychodynamics, mental illness, unconscious processes, degrees of pathology, defensive mechanisms (e.g., Chrzanowski, 1977, 1978, 1980; Michels, 1977; Millon, 1981; Saretsky, 1981). It is easy to speak about "their" orally regressive neurotic features, their repressed infantile fears, their passive aggressivity, their terror of intimacy and closeness, their needs for acting out or intimidation or control or provoked counter-aggression. It is easy to search and find commonalities in their demographic features, their history of hospitalization, their responses to treatment (Glatzer, 1972; Millon, 1981; Neill, 1979; Robbins, Stern, Robbins & Margolin, 1978; Robertiello & Forbes, 1970; Saretsky, 1981).

The locus and therapeutic data of the experiential therapist mean that there is little or no place for engaging in an external antagonistic stance against the patient, having to do something to combat the abrasive patient, or seeing it as a problem/symptom which must be treated.

There Is a Carrying Forward of the Abrasiveness and Also of the Deeper Experiencing

What does the experiential therapist do with the abrasiveness? How is it used in the course of therapeutic work? To begin with, the abrasiveness is experienced more, and so too is whatever deeper experiencing underlies it. When the patient is being and experiencing abrasiveness, and when the therapist is experiencing this along with the patient, then there is a carrying forward of the abrasiveness, and there is a carrying forward of whatever experiencing is present but deeper. They are welcomed, fostered, helped along, disclosed, enlivened, expressed, given heightened depth and breadth, amplitude, and saturation.

In a recent situation with neighbors, or in a remote situation with the neighborhood kids, the patient and therapist are letting the abrasiveness happen more fully. They are in an experiential state of being petty martinets. If the deeper experiencing is that of being a nonentity, that too is carried forward so that patient and therapist share in its heightened experiencing. One therapeutic use of the abrasiveness is to carry forward the experiencing of it, and the experiencing of whatever lies deeper.

There Is Integrative Encountering Between the Abrasive Patient and the Deeper Experiencing

A second therapeutic use of the abrasiveness is to bring about a thorough encounter between the abrasive patient and the patient's own deeper experiencing. In this encounter, the therapist merges into the identity of this deeper experiencing, and serves as its voice. It is as if the patient's own deeper experiencing comes alive, has a voice, and is more than willing to tangle with the abrasive patient in an all-out encounter. It heats up with a feelinged interrelationship between the abusive, menacing patient and the deeper experiencing of the being a nothing, a nonentity or whatever is the nature of the deeper experiencing. From there it moves in the direction of a head-on collision, a clashing having-it-out with one another.

The inexorable consequence is movement in the direction of an integrative relationship between the abrasive patient and the deeper experiencing. By "integrative" I mean that the patient is much more welcoming toward the deeper experiencing; I mean that the patient is and feels much more harmonious and intimate and easy with it; I mean that the very content and nature of the deeper experiencing undergoes a radical shift toward its good form, its integrated form. No longer a monstrous state of nothingness, a screeching hell of nonexistence, it may now transform into, perhaps, a new-found letting-be, a whole new experiencing of not having to prove, a calm inner strength of merely existing.

There Is Disengagement From the Abrasive Person and Entry Into Being the Deeper Experiencing

Now the patient is invited to disengage from being the person who is abusive, who must threaten and menace others, and to enter into being the person who is the deeper experiencing. If the patient is ready and willing, the therapist shows the patient how to do this. It means a radical shift, a wholesale disengagement from the person who is abrasive, who must be abrasive. It means that the very heart of the very core of the sense of I-ness is to enter into being the deeper personality which may be absolute nothingness, a nonexisting vacuum; or it may be a wonderful inner strength of merely existing, a marvelously peaceful letting-be. Whatever the nature and content of the deeper experiencing, the patient is now being this identity, and is no longer the person who is abrasive.

There Is an Experiential Consideration of New Ways of Being in the Extra-Therapy World

In each session the final step invites the patient to live in the extra-therapy world, the real world of today and next week and thereafter. Furthermore, the patient is invited to consider the radical possibility of being and behaving in qualitatively new ways, of building and constructing qualitatively new worlds. We face the experiential reality of really being different, really behaving in new ways which pack a consequential punch. We face the real meaning of being a new and changing person in a world which is significantly changed. The patient gets an experiential taste of a powerfully real change which may be exciting or scary, may include slight behavioral fine tuning or dramatic shifts in living out one's life. It may consist of daring new ways of being or letting go of outworn and problematic chunks of one's life. The changes in one's way of being and in one's extra-therapy world may be serious or playful, limited or far-reaching, extravagant or mundane, realistic or unrealistic, the expression of heaven or hell.

WHAT HAPPENS TO THE ABRASIVENESS?

If our frame of reference is a single session, then here is what happens to the abrasiveness: (a) There is some carrying forward of the actual experiencing of the abrasiveness itself and perhaps also whatever experiencing underlies the abrasiveness. (b) There is some integrative softening and welcoming in the relationship between whatever is the deeper experiencing and the abrasive person. (c) There is a measure of disengagement from being the person who is abrasive, and at least some moments of entering into being the person who is the deeper experiencing. (d) There is a consideration (an experiential taste) of being a qualitatively new and different person in a new and different world. Now let us step back and ask what may happen to the abrasiveness over the course of sessions.

If the patient chooses, from the very beginning, to be abusive toward the therapist, to be antagonistic and challenging and menacing at the therapist, then therapeutic work does not start and this therapy is inappropriate. The abrasiveness remains. Experiential therapy is wholly inappropriate, useless, and ineffective with patients who do not undertake therapeutic work. That is the patient's choice, and that is the way the experiential method works. However, if the patient undertakes experiential work, and if it is the being and experiencing of abrasiveness which is front and center, session after session, then the principles of experiential psychotherapy indicate that there is always the risk of two directions of change.

One is that the abrasiveness may wash away. The patient risks no longer being a person who is this way. It is gone, let go. As the patient undertakes the carrying forward of the abrasiveness and of the deeper experiencing, the whole foundation crumbles. As the patient undergoes integrative relationships with the deeper experiencing, the abrasiveness atrophies. As the patient disengages from being the person who is abrasive, and enters into being the deeper experiencing, the abrasiveness is let go. As the patient experiences the real considering of whole new ways of being in a whole new extra-therapy world, the abrasiveness fades away. The risk is that the abrasiveness may wash away.

The other risk is that a different kind of abrasiveness will flourish. There is a qualitative transformation in its content. It becomes a sound and honest toughness, a playful forthrightness, a powerful ability to confront, a pleasant curmudgeonness, an aggressive leadership, a disarmingly open spiritedness, an unwavering dedication, a delightful sparring, a lovely closeness and intimacy. The risk is that it will no longer require an external target, and that person will be replaced with a world constructed to provide for the new experience into which the abrasiveness is transformed. If the abrasiveness remains, its nature and content will undergo change into its integrative form, and the encompassing world will symmetrically be changed to provide for the new kind of experiencing. Through experiential care and feeding, the former abrasiveness either washes away or undergoes transformation into something which can no longer be described as abrasiveness.

REFERENCES

Chrzanowski, G. (1977). Interpersonal treatment method with the difficult patient. In B. B. Wolman (Ed.), *International encyclopedia of neurology, psychiatry, psychoanalysis, and psychology.* New York: Aesculapius.

Chrzanowski, G. (1978). Malevolent transformation and the negative therapeutic reaction. *Contemporary Psychoanalysis, 14*, 405-413.

Chrzanowski, G. (1980). Problem patients or troublemakers? Dynamic and therapeutic considerations. *American Journal of Psychotherapy, 34*, 26-38.

Fromm, M. G. (1981). Impasse and transitional relatedness. In T. Saretsky (Ed.), *Resolving treatment impasses: The difficult patient* (pp. 5-29). New York: Human Sciences Press.

Glatzer, H. T. (1972). Treatment of oral character neurosis in group therapy. In C. Sager & H. Kaplan (Eds.), *Progress in group and family therapy.* New York: Brunner/Mazel.

Mahrer, A. R. (1983). *Experiential psychotherapy: Basic practices.* New York: Brunner/Mazel.

Michels, R. (1977). Treatment of the difficult patient in psychotherapy. *Canadian Psychiatric Association Journal, 22*, 117-121.

Millon, T. (1981). *Disorders of personality: DSM III, Axis II.* New York: Wiley.

Neill, J. R. (1979). The difficult patient: Identification and response. *Journal of Clinical Psychiatry, 40*, 209-212.

Robbins, E., Stern, M., Robbins, L., & Margolin, L. (1978). Unwelcome patients: Where can they find asylum? *Hospital and Community Psychiatry, 29*, 44-46.

Robertiello, R., & Forbes, S. (1970). The treatment of the masochistic character disorder. *Journal of Contemporary Psychotherapy, 2*, 3-12.

Rosen, V. (1955). The reconstruction of a traumatic childhood event in a case of derealization. *Journal of the American Psychoanalytic Association, 3*, 211-221.

Saretsky, T. (1981). *Resolving treatment impasses: The difficult patient.* New York: Human Sciences Press.

West, W. Jr. (1978). Combined approaches in the treatment of the orally regressed masochistic character disorder. *Journal of Contemporary Psychotherapy, 9*, 155-161.

A Malicious Sense of Survival

Reuven Bar-Levav

Paul came immediately to mind when I contemplated writing this article on the abrasive patient. He was such an obnoxious, difficult, and unfriendly man in his thirties, handsome but bear-like, and what was most typical about him was his sullenness. Did he ever smile, even once, during our 8-years' association? He was always serious, he walked slowly, he trusted nobody, and when he was hurt or scared he would attack viciously those who were nearest to him. He was very bright and his verbal attacks upon me and upon members of his psychotherapy group were always delivered in a calm and excessively deliberate manner, as if he were above the scuffle and not touchable by us. Since he was so very sensitive and so very scared he had developed a special capacity to detect and to remember everyone's Achilles' heel, and he used it well. He would pounce only at the right moment, almost never impulsively, in a slow and merciless manner, upon any real shortcoming of the other. Instinctively he attempted to establish a psychologic *cordon sanitaire* around him, a safe zone into which no one was allowed and, therefore, no one could hurt him. He fully expected to be damaged by anyone, anywhere, always. He was exceedingly sensitive to embarrassment, shame, and humiliation. Even an innocent or friendly remark was often misinterpreted by him as having a secret, hostile intent. He had serious difficulties with his self-image and his sexual identification, and in a paranoid-like way, he was sure that others actually saw him as a distorted and worthless creature. From his point of view he merely lashed back at his enemies who would always, as a matter of course, attack and belittle him, as if he were less than a person.

Why did he stay in individual therapy with me so long and how could he tolerate being in a psychotherapy group? In spite of the obvious psychopathology, he also had a great deal of strength. These islands of health brought him to treatment in the first place, and they maintained him there

Reuven Bar-Levav, M.D., came to medicine from the social sciences, with undergraduate and graduate degrees in economics and political science. His medical degree is from Wayne State University (1962) where he also had his internship and residency in psychiatry. Dr. Bar-Levav has developed a personality theory which will soon appear in book form under the title, *Just Below the Angels*. He has also developed a new system of intensive psychotherapy known as Crisis Mobilization Therapy, which is based on this theory.

in spite of all the hardships. But beyond that he was also a very stubborn man, not one to give in or to yield under pressure, no matter how extreme. It was far too humiliating to do so. He would not allow himself to be seen in such a light under any circumstances. So, he stuck it out, month after month, year after year, as I did also.

But why did I stick with him? This question surfaced quite naturally as I was dictating these notes, for it seemed even to me as I was describing Paul that only a masochistic person full of self-hate would agree to work under such difficult and degrading circumstances. I did not need him to earn a living, so why did I do it? Because my experiences with Paul were not really so difficult and they were never degrading. Although he could look at me, almost snake-like, with cold eyes and with venom in his mouth and hurl invectives at me that were extreme and indecent under other circumstances, it usually did not cause me pain, nor was I scared or insulted by him.

I do not assume a detached position vis-à-vis my patients, and I did not with Paul. I also did not hide behind the mantle of being a professional and did not dismiss him as a crazy person whose words to not count for much. In fact, I respected his great intelligence, and I even managed to like him somehow. My work with people requires that we form a real and involving relationship, one in which I do not merely sell my time but where I also give of myself. If I did not respect and like him in spite of all his antics, I could not do what needed to be done. It would have become obvious after a very short lapse of time that my words were empty and that my presence was only as-if. Of all my patients Paul would have detected this earlier than most, for his distrust and his intuitive suspiciousness were exceedingly well developed, indeed. But he did stay for 8 long years, and I remember many instances of looking forward to his sessions with me. What made this possible?

As I was contemplating this question, I first thought that the answer would be found in the theoretical model to which I adhere and which serves as the basis for my work with patients. The model is a medical one, and according to it, I, a physician and an expert, am making myself available for the treatment of illnesses of those human beings who come to me. Paul's obnoxious and hostile manner was part of his illness, unpleasant as is the stench of a festering flesh wound or the bowel movements of an old or dying patient unable to control his anus. I don't have to like it, but I can't blame the patient for it.

Paul was often not a pleasant patient, but then, in this model, I have no right to expect pleasantness, although I always welcome it. All that my patients owe me is a fair compensation for my time; I cannot and should not expect appreciation, gratification, gratitude, or love. When these are offered, as they often are, they are bonuses that I am very happy about. My sincerest efforts on behalf of my patients cannot be conditional upon receiving them. Old-time and hard-working physicians who treated with equal devotion and conscientiousness battlefield casualties of both camps served as my models when I fashioned my professional identity. I am perhaps old-fashioned, but I still do not regard being a physician as merely a good way of making a living and surely not as a business. I still believe that it imposes upon me an obligation to do my best for every human being, regardless of color, creed, political persuasion, or nationality. Human beings really are a miracle of creation, and they must be treated respectfully as such; their pain and suffering must be minimized, their welfare and health maximized.

This theoretical model and my professional identity as a physician surely helped me when I worked with Paul. These views of myself and of others have become over the years more than mere beliefs that I held on to. They have become an integral part of my personality and value system, and they helped me in difficult moments with Paul. I continued to maintain my objectivity and my detachment from the accusations and the invectives that he repeatedly hurled against me, without detaching or distancing myself from really being involved with him, the person throwing such accusations directly at my face.

This, however, was not the entire story. I also remembered the teachings of my old professor of psychiatry, John Dorsey, who had impressed upon me many years ago that everyone does the very best one can, that if one only could one would surely do better. I am not so sure even now whether my old professor meant this only as an explanation or also as an alibi, but for me it was always an important reminder that even obnoxious characteristics are a person's self-helpful ways of existing in the world. For me at least, it is always merely an explanation, not an excuse, and it helps me remain nonjudgmental and noncritical, at least in the clinical setting, even in the face of extreme provocation. It also helps me to accept in that setting that which would otherwise be unacceptable.

Such an acceptance of obnoxious ways of being is in any event limited and welcome only as long as it remains confined to verbal or vocal expressions, and only if it is not actually manifested in actions or in behavior. What I was willing and able to tolerate from Paul is unacceptable to me when it comes even from a close relative in a social situation.

Hysterical and/or obnoxious behavior in such a setting is very embarrassing to less-disturbed friends and relatives who must witness it, and they often try to minimize their embarrassment by appeasing the obnoxious person with the hope of cutting the outbursts short. Such appeasement is as futile in personal as it is in political relationships, and it always breeds tragedy in the long run. Munich did not avert World War II. No healthy relationship, therapeutic or otherwise, can survive unless it is based on mutual respect and on mutual regard, at least for the physical safety of both parties and for the setting in which they find themselves.

Most long-term relationships are, unfortunately, held together by a different glue: fear of loneliness and of abandonment.

Psychiatrists and other mental health professionals often err in assuming that since they understand the unconscious roots and motivations of behavior better than others, therefore it naturally follows that they should also advocate excusing anti-social acts. After all, they always have over-determined causes. If it is true, the argument goes, that every person does the very best he or she can, then how can anyone be blamed for their failures or be held responsible for them?

Such a line of reasoning is based on a fundamental fallacy. It focuses so totally on the individual that it overlooks the existence of a society which has a responsibility to all its members to protect them from being forced by some. Even acts committed because of irresistible forces within an individual have social consequences. The deep daily involvement of mental health professionals with individual human beings in distress and the intimate knowledge they have of their pain and suffering has blinded many of them to the fact that we all live in social contexts. The very survival of societies may dictate the taking of steps that limit an individual's freedom to act according to his or her wishes or needs. The Bill of Human Rights is unenforceable if it guarantees conflicting rights to individuals living together. In practice, it is and must be limited by the requirements of societal living, even in the absence of a Bill of Societal Rights. Because of the tendency to confuse understanding with excusing a person's acts, many psychiatrists and psychotherapists have in the past assumed "liberal" positions as if by a knee-jerk reflex, even when such positions made absolutely no sense. This is part of the reason why our professional image is relatively so low.

Aside from his verbal attacks, Paul's behavior toward members of his psychotherapy group and toward me was essentially correct and proper. He adhered strictly to our non-acting-out contract. He was both too afraid to grossly act out, for he knew that this would not be tolerated and he did not wish to risk our relationship, and he was also too healthy to act crazily. This made it possible for him and for me to maintain our long association and to continue our long struggle. The volleys of his invectives may have been extreme and his denunciations of me and of others were often sharp and expressed in the strongest terms, but he was, nevertheless, respectful at all times of the rules of our contract. Obviously there were no violent acts and no threats of such. He usually came on time and canceled appropriately; he paid as agreed upon; he was willing and able to consider and to examine post-factum the meaning of his behavior; and when not hurt or afraid he was often thoughtful and openly introspective. But what really made it possible for me to stay the course and even to look forward to being with him was the clear definition of my own ego boundaries.

I never ignore what people, including my patients, tell me about my-

self, and I always try to examine as well as I can how valid both their accusations and their compliments are. I suspect the motives of those who
hate and vilify me no more than those who love and adore me. I generally find that there is no smoke without fire, and that in spite of inaccura-
cies there generally is a grain of truth to be found in everything. What en-
ables me to examine even painful and difficult words is my ability to
sustain myself and to not excessively need the approval of others for
maintaining my self-respect and my sense of self-worth. I wish for approval, acceptance, and love, and I am happier when I get them, but I
survive reasonably well for long periods of time without getting them
from others, since I am usually able to give them to myself. In the absence of confirmation from others I try to find resources within myself to
nourish me, even under conditions of some stress. I essentially know
where I begin and where I end, what is me and what is not, what is inside
and what is outside of me.

Since I have worked on sprucing up and clarifying the boundaries of
my self over several decades through much painful self-observation and
self-scrutiny, some of the accusations that Paul hurled against me have
found their target, but many have clearly been mere expressions of his
need to keep me at a safe distance. They had little to do with my real being. I always tried to ask myself whether he had caught me at a moment
of inner tension or weakness, but I could also ascertain when he was off
the mark. Most often he wanted to push me aside when he experienced
my intimate involvement with him as an unwelcome intrusion upon his
life-space. This he sensed as a wish on my part to diminish him, to swal-
low him, to cause him to no longer be separate as an individual. Such
horrible fears of engulfment or of nonbeing were obviously based on very
early pre-verbal sensations of the infant within him, but only rarely did I
interpret them. Right or wrong, in the midst of fear such interpretations
are of no value.

If Paul was to be helped beyond the point where he existed it would be
through our real relationship, through his increasing knowledge that I was
not the way he perceived me. His earliest caretakers, especially his
mother, were probably experienced as wishing to "take him over," but
this was another age, and he already understood all this cognitively. What
he needed to do was to actually experience himself as an adult, no longer
the infant. He was competent and capable, intelligent and sensitive, except that he himself was the last to know it.

Noah Webster defined abrasive as something that tends to provoke anger and ill will. Abrasion is an aggressively irritating action, caused by a
rough substance such as sandpaper. This is how Paul intended to be. An
abrasive substance causes a wearing off and a grinding down of that
which it rubs against; it can scrape the skin and the feelings of those not
so secure within their own boundaries. Whenever a patient is experi-

enced, or is described, as abrasive, it always indicates that he or she succeeded in aggressively acting upon the therapist. The patient merely does what he or she unconsciously senses as necessary for survival, but if this provokes anger and ill will then it signifies a breakdown in the therapeutic relationship. It must be repaired or ended. Repair means that the therapist must attend to the task of shoring up his or her own ego boundaries, a difficult but necessary process that requires time and much effort.

As long as the therapeutic contract is adhered to, no abrasive patients should theoretically ever exist, except in the perception of therapists whose sense of self is shaky. Attacks upon the person of the therapist are perceived as dangerous ad hominem attacks only in the absence of clear ego boundaries. When the boundaries are fuzzy such fear of attrition of the self can be stimulated even by sharp professional interchanges, which explains why so much boring double-talk and vaguely worded criticism typifies most scientific meetings.

The treatment of the abrasive patient requires, therefore, first and foremost, that the therapist define his or her own self as clearly as possible. The task of separation-individuation must essentially be completed before the work with such difficult patients can get under way. Verbal attacks of any intensity would then no longer be a cause of alarm to the therapist, and none would cause him or her to lose the perspective of reality.

Only once over a period of two decades or so of working intensively with many people have I been threatened physically by a patient. A Vietnam veteran over 6 feet tall that I had been seeing individually and in a group came into my office one day, pulled out a large knife from his boot, and cut my telephone wire. He was angry and disappointed and told me that he was not getting his way in therapy and that we surely wouldn't be interrupted once the phone was dead. I would now have to listen to all his complaints and correct the situation. I would surely hear him now, he claimed, a thing he believed was normally not true. He himself was able to recognize soon that I had treated him decently and consistently; in reality he was still sitting on my couch, knife in hand, telling me not to scream because "by the time they come I could cut your throat." I induced him finally to throw his knife to the far corner of the room and immediately stopped my work with him.

This man was obviously not an abrasive patient; his act was not an irritation but an actual threat. Patients who are described as abrasive are not violent; they are merely chronically unpleasant, a pain to be with, a repeated drain on one's energies.

Why are they this way? Because this was their most effective way to relate to the mothering person during the earliest period of their lives. They were perhaps colicky babies. Their abrasive traits are their trademark, their identity, their way of being-in-the-world. They had found themselves a niche within their families as irritants, trouble makers, dour and sour, unpleasant and unhappy creatures, sometimes loud-mouths, sometimes pouters, eternally unsatisfiable. Not many smiles, not much joy, but plenty of complaints and bitterness. What is abrasive to others helps them find a little security and comfort. Without their abrasive traits they would experience themselves as totally naked and powerless to affect those around them; they would not even be recognized. Without their abrasive traits, they fear, nobody would attend to, or care for, them; they would not only be overlooked but also forgotten. Most important, being abrasive is their way of making contact. Being abrasive also provides them with a wonderful way of continuously testing their relationships. Each time they are not turned out into the cold, not rejected, confirms to them that they are worthy, still welcome, loved. As such, being abrasive is a necessity for feeling safe. It must not be given up.

Since most human beings, including psychotherapists, are far from finished in their task of individuating, the boundaries of the self are often somewhat soft and ill-defined. Having had a long analysis or even an extensive course of intensive psychotherapy does not guarantee that the urgent hunger for confirmation from the environment has been eliminated. Abrasive patients are, therefore, a very real and heavy burden for most therapists who often eventually reject them and pronounce them as unanalyzable, incurable, and hopeless. A therapist may find it very difficult to stay with a patient unless he or she shows signs of getting well or at least of making good progress, which the therapist may need as an antidote for a sense of powerlessness. When the patient not only seems to be stuck but is also battering the therapist verbally, when he or she rubs the therapist the wrong way, as any irritant would, it is easy to tire of the task. The relationship is often allowed to die if the patient does not leave first, or it is actually terminated by the therapist. In either case it confirms the pathologic expectation of the patient that he or she is unworthy and would always be rejected eventually.

Each failure of this kind rigidifies and fixes the maladaptive defensive structure even more, and both patient and therapist unwittingly and unconsciously become partners to this self-fulfilling prophesy. Recognizing this unconscious collusion may help therapists stay with these patients in spite of the difficulties. Avoidable tragedies will thus occur less often.

The use of combined individual and group psychotherapy has been found to be one way of diluting the damaging effects to a relationship that an abrasive patient presents. Since the abrasive qualities interfere with the formation of a close relationship, it is at best difficult to get such a patient intimately involved in a one-to-one relationship. A psychotherapy group in which he or she does not become scapegoated can become a relatively safe setting in which provocative engagements are minimized, since this setting allows the patient to titrate the distance between himself and others. Sufficient distance can thus be created also between the patient and his or her pathology, which facilitates self-observation. This is a necessary first step before the willingness to engage in the more difficult work of character reorganization can be mobilized.

A therapist who might not be able to submit to repeated assaults in the dyadic setting alone may well find it possible to continue working with an abrasive patient in combined individual and group therapy, since in the latter other humans provide reality reminders about the therapist's position and worth. This should ideally not be necessary, but in practice the presence of others during repeated episodes in which the patient inveighs, denounces, denunciates, rails against, and scolds the therapist (or another patient) forces a greater measure of reality into this distorted situation. It also helps both the abrasive patient and those attacked by him or her from losing perspective altogether.

Although such a patient may put a heavy burden on the functioning of a psychotherapy group, the presence of two such patients in any one group sometimes makes it easier for both and for the remaining group members. Each one of these abrasive patients may be blind to his or her own distortions for a long time, but they are usually able to see without too much difficulty how another person with similar psychopathological adjustments distorts reality. This speeds up the process and helps the distorting patient to also become aware of his or her own pathology more easily. Contrary to widespread belief, such awareness is not curative in itself, but it is a step in the right direction.

Patients who appear as abrasive are essentially extremely scared people, very sensitive and very hurt. Their typical ways of being help them maintain sufficient distance between themselves and others. This, however, is only one side of their personality, for in having lived this way throughout life they also find themselves in a state of extreme loneliness, and they usually also experience tremendously powerful yearnings for closeness, contact, and acceptance. This paradoxical and tragic contradiction often leads to suicide. The apparent provocative anger which they display in all close relationships also serves as a defense against these powerful yearnings, which they commonly deny because they are so terrifying.

Therapists who discover within themselves the stamina, and who possess sufficiently well-defined boundaries, will discover that working with these patients is a most rewarding human experience which literally saves lives. By a lucky coincidence, I recently discovered an audiotape made with Paul's permission during one of the last hours before he left therapy with me. He terminated before his work was finished, in part because of external circumstances, and the termination was somewhat abrupt, as the following transcript shows. Not having remembered the existence of this tape since it was originally made several years ago, I was deeply touched as I finally listened to it in preparation for writing this article.

My basic memory residue of our long relationship consisted of the many confrontations and of the sullenness to which I had been repeatedly subjected in such a merciless fashion. I also remembered his sensitivity and his pain, but I did not remember sufficiently well how very loving he also was. The tape reminded me. The transcription is accurate but for several deletions, and yet, like all transcripts, it fails to convey the voice quality, its quivering or his soft sobbing when he was deeply touched. But here it is, anyway.

Paul: You know, [slowly, softly, thoughtfully] what I feel sad about, for myself, is that on the one hand I am a little suspicious. I also don't see enough of the other person's agenda and what they do, and I see so much of it as a reaction to me, or a failure on my part.

RBL: Yes, it is your tendency to do so. [Long silence] Before we go further, there is one week in December in which I won't be here, the week of December 8th, and I already told you so. But the following week I cannot be here on Wednesday afternoon, could you come on Wednesday morning?

Paul: Well, that brings up something I was going to talk about today, sooner or later. I don't think I will be able to come to therapy after the end of this month.

RBL: [Surprised] You mean at the end of November?

Paul: The end of November, right.

RBL: Okay, talk about that.

Paul: Well, plain and simple, I don't have any more money.

RBL: That is plain and simple.

Paul: [After pause] But that doesn't mean that there are not a lot of feelings, and it is not the way I would want to do it. [Pause] What it amounts to is that at the end of this month I run out of money.

RBL: So, this is it, it is over?

Paul: Well, you know, in a way that is going to be it, but on the other hand, it isn't something that I have not known about for a while. And it has had a bearing on the way I act, the way I think, and the way I react, and how scared I get. So, kind of by myself, I have been living the end of my therapy.

RBL: Why by yourself?

Paul: Well, partly, [pause] I don't know, I didn't like to bring it up in group because I was afraid the people would, you know, I was afraid of what I considered people's reaction, and I was concerned that I also might be little hysterical, might be overplaying this money stuff. [Pause] And, I kept thinking, figuring out what I could do and how I could do, and I kept looking at my feelings. And, why I didn't bring it up to you, I guess—oh, any number of reasons, I guess I am not entirely sure why. I kept thinking that maybe I would borrow the money. The more I think about it, I don't want to involve my wife, you know that I am dependent upon her . . . if I was really to go and say, "I'm really, *really* crazy, I can't live without therapy. I'm going to borrow the money," maybe I could get her to co-sign, you know I don't have a job now—but it's too distasteful for me, so I am not going to do it. [Silence] You know, I say all this against the background of maybe I can change my mind. I am hesitant to sound in absolutes, but all things considered this is my current position.

RBL: I'm glad you don't sound too absolute.

Paul: Because I got a vague—I got a pretty good, it is not so vague—idea where my craziness is, and there are things to work on—you know, I hurt so easy, I color my relationships the way I just described—those are the two big things. When I get hurt, I get angry, and beyond that, which doesn't come up so often in here, I really judge myself harshly. Those are three big areas. One that I don't talk much about, that I try to sneak into the group lately, one which I reflect on a lot, is how over the years . . . [pause] But in all areas, my life has improved . . . I even enjoy lately the idea of, I mean, I like my fantasy of my being a little leaner, maybe meaner looking, my hair shorter, my face more . . . a kind of leaner, more wiry-looking guy who could just call some woman up and say, you know, "I saw you today, and I would like to be with you tonight, tomorrow night," whatever, you know.

RBL: To meet you . . .

Paul: Yeah, to meet you. I'd like to sleep with you. I'd like to take you to London. I'll spend money on you. I'll make you happy for 3 days, you make me happy for 3 days. You know, not heavy, not let's get married and have babies, forever, not that type of stuff, (pause) that's new, to be free to think this way . . .

RBL: That's new.

Paul: Yes, and I like it. [12-second pause] Those are some of the feelings. Some of the other feelings are really sad, about [silence] there are a lot of things between us that aren't really said. From me to you in any case, and I wish [voice faltering] I had the time to say it. I'm afraid of being [pause] ah well, [pause] but I am also very appreciative. I didn't want to rush into this, because sometimes I think I am not done fighting with you, but . . . I don't think I can fight still.

RBL: One does not preclude the other.

Paul: Another good thing is that in the time I fight with you I can find now, that even though what I believe are things that I don't like about you are not reasons for killing you, or [pause] I am able to expand the concept of you, around those things, and I don't feel that I have to give up certain things, compromise myself, I am able to see many good things about you [said with a voice in a low register—trying to control his voice while saying these words].

RBL: The world is not so black and white. I am not.

Paul: Yes, it is not an either/or situation, and yet I don't compromise my fierceness or my intensity—I'm just bigger.

RBL: Loving doesn't make you weak, in other words.

Paul: No it doesn't. But beyond that, it would appear it is bigger than that. [Pause] That is certainly true. [5-second silence] Yeah, it is bigger, loving is bigger. [25-second silence]

RBL: ?

Paul: . . . eight years, and then to say good-bye in 3 weeks, [with pain in his voice] it is so hard. Eight years of fighting, and three weeks of not . . .

RBL: [With slight chuckle] We're not sure about that yet, but there was lots of loving in the past, too. [Sounds as if there are tears in the therapist's eyes also]

Paul: Well, not like . . . now [with tears]. I have always been very careful not to admit that I loved you, in public. I was always careful to say things precisely about you which I believed . . . in other words the truth about you. [12-second silence] In effect, I was disowning you, although I would say good things about you. Now, even if someone else would say things that were not good about you, and I believed them to be true, I think that I would still not disown you.

RBL: That's good for both of us. Mostly, for you. You are big enough that you can do that. [10-second delay] You got guts, it takes a man, not a boy. [33-second delay] If you really leave, Paul, I will miss you. I don't know if you will really leave at the end of the month or not, but I will surely miss you if you go. It is also 8 years of my life. [24-second silence]

Paul: [Large breath of air taken by Paul, hardly audible] It's been a long time. [12-second silence]

RBL: Your life really changed, huh?

Paul: I think it has. I have given it a lot of thought in the last 6 to 8 months. And in many ways I am the same, the same core person, but different. Not in opposition, but different. [12-second silence]

RBL: The core may not be the same either. It may not be all done, but it is not the same. You forget how you were when you came here. You were very far from being a man.

Paul: That's true, that's very true. [20-second silence] I came up with, in my mind a lot of deals to make, this last [pause] but I am ashamed of all the deals that I have made in the past, in which I made myself small, had people take care of me, I don't want to do that anymore.

RBL: It would be better if you didn't have to leave, because this is the first time that you really are much more flexible in regards to people. It shows especially in your group. [Pause] Somebody told me, only yesterday, that it was a pleasure to see some of the things you did to help another person, and you did it not as if you were a detached therapist, although it was nice therapy too, but as one human being would be with another, without leaving yourself out. I wasn't there, I didn't see it, but it didn't surprise me, and I was pleased to hear it. [Pause] So, this is so new for you, and you may not get much support for that kind of living, in a less defensive way. You may not have a chance to express yourself this way much, to develop it much, plus all the other things that you mentioned earlier. So, it would be good for you if you could stay and finish the job. But . . . it is also good to see where you have come from.

Paul: Well, I hear what you are saying. I am sad because I know it is true. But I am ashamed . . . [silence]

RBL: I am not trying to influence you to stay. I don't know what the solution is. It may be more useful for you, if there is no honorable way for you to stay, that you leave. Perhaps you'll come back sometime. Maybe you ought to take a year's vacation. I don't know what, just it is such an inopportune time because you are so deeply and differently involved. . . . I am not suggesting that you compromise your dignity. [Pause] If there is a dignified way of staying that would be best. You compromised your dignity a lot, and I am glad that you are sensitive to it now. I am glad that you don't want to stay at any cost. [14-second silence] You are still living in sort of a desert, at home, at school, in terms of open, reasonably loving and trusting human relationships in which there is mutuality, no compromises based on fears, there is dignity . . . [pause]

Paul: I know what you are saying. It may sound strange . . .

RBL: Why strange?

Paul: Well, so many people don't know what all this means . . . and many people know the words, but they don't know what they really mean. [13-second silence] If I were afraid I wouldn't survive in this desert, I would pay the price of dignity.

RBL: Yeah.

Paul: I mean that this is not the Garden of Eden, but it is not the middle of the desert either.

RBL: You are likely to survive in the desert, because you are a hardy plant. It is just that it would be nice if you didn't have to fall back on your hardy-plant-living so much. It would be nice if conditions were better.

Paul: That is interesting, because lately, I don't think of myself so much as a hardy plant any more. I know that I take sustenance for myself, I don't see myself as getting it from anybody else. I mean, except that I get it from you.

RBL: Not even from me so much. You find a place with me, near me, with me, in which you can draw on yourself, without having to distort yourself much.

Paul: [Slowly, quietly] That's true.

RBL: I'm not giving you so much as I am providing you a place to flex your muscles. And to experience your tenderness. [Pause]

Paul: I have given that a lot of thought lately, why, you know, the way I react so I don't have to show my tenderness. I guess I am afraid, if I am tender, I won't survive. And yet, my tenderness is such a big part of me, so when I act tough, I hide such a big part of me.

RBL: And the best part of you. The toughness you had all along, but it wasn't tempered with your softness. [45-second silence]

Paul: My marriage, it is like a desert, too, really, I mean, it is a good analogy. My wife is very loving, very kind, she works her ass off. I say to myself, the reason is that she is afraid . . . she is very loving.

RBL: The reason for what?

Paul: The reason she is what she is. The reason that she acts the way she acts. She is loving, there is a part of her that is loving. I'm sad, maybe I'm wrong, maybe it's not justifiable, but I see her in some ways as a little girl, trying very hard to do what is right. She does it because it is right. [Pause] We are together, but we are apart. I am reluctant to say anything really definitive, in case it is me. [20-second silence]

RBL: What happens when you are sensitive and tender with her?

Paul: She likes that.

RBL: Does she respond to you?

Paul: Yeah.

RBL: Well, that's good. Why do you call it desert?

Paul: Well, it is almost as though, the way I see it, everything important to me, I mean, psychology, and therapy, and people's feelings, and why they do things, she just thinks that is all a crock of shit. I mean, she tolerates me.

RBL: You can't talk to her?

Paul: I can't talk to her about everything, about anything like that.

RBL: Have you tried?

Paul: Yeah.

RBL: So, if you come enthusiastically with something that happened to you, she is unreceptive?

Paul: That's right . . . [46-second silence]

RBL: Do you talk openly?

Paul: Not about psychology. No.

RBL: Not about psychology. About yourself, about your feelings, about your life, your hopes, your aspirations, your fears, not psychology . . . that sounds like a college course. Or about her feelings, about her aspirations, her wishes.

Paul: Well, what happens is that she doesn't usually talk about her feelings or her wishes until she gets very, very tired, and she goes to a meeting and they tell her that she has to come in on Saturday, then she tells me the details of how she involves herself. The way I see it, I see her as technically expert and sophisticated in many ways, but very vulnerable to the cunning of some of the men she works with. It is almost as if she can be trapped into doing more, to the point of where she is spread so thin. I worry about her, and when I try to show her how she does this, she gets angry.

RBL: At you?

Paul: Yeah. She says, "You're full of shit. Every God-damned thing I try to do, you turn into something, nothing is ever simple, it always has some reason underneath. Can't you ever just listen to me?"

RBL: She can't see that you are motivated by a wish to help her. A loving wish to help her?

Paul: Right, that is my belief. She does not see me as having a loving wish to help her. As a matter of fact, that is her major complaint because I do not just sit there and listen, in other words, provide a listening ear, without any kind of comment. That is her reason for saying that I don't love her, that I don't give a shit, and that I don't care about anybody except myself. That record is being played out about every 11 weeks. It is harsh perhaps to say that. . . . I've never been able to really get her, have her, believe that I am really on her side. Lately, I have just cut right in and asked her, "Do you really believe that I am on your side?". . . . the other day, we had a very harsh argument about the way we treat—each of us treats—the kids. I was very angry, because I believe she is always annoyed. When she gets hard, she is annoyed. Our daughter can't do anything right. And I am very afraid that she could be in a lot of trouble . . . [Long silence] We scream at each other . . . she is a rigid, unyielding, very afraid young woman. Not so young anymore. I told her the other day that if she didn't start changing, I told her, "You know what? It is going to be very tough for us to die, married to each other." [Short silence] I didn't want to talk to you about her.

RBL: You are not talking about her, you are talking about yourself. Your disappointment, your hurt. . . . You are looking at yourself at this moment not critically, with a sense that you have done all that one can do.

Paul: [Pause] Yeah, I've done a lot, I mean honest effort is an easy way to describe it. I really made it work. I am ashamed of some things, you know, I am ashamed that I don't work and earn money now. But I sure looked into myself and changed myself.

RBL: She is really not changing?

Paul: No. [Pause] In some ways she is. I am telling you the problem parts, but my wife is shifting. [9-second pause] She doesn't act on her impulses like I do . . . she has been able to make some shifts out of sheer will.

RBL: Also because she is a little less scared when you are less threatening.

Paul: That could well be true. She is more relaxed socially, you know what I mean. That must be because I'm picking up the slack. She is more open and shows more of herself. And she is not ashamed of herself. There are some parts that if they were me, I would be ashamed, and I look at her and see that she is more open. Not that I would be rightfully ashamed, but ashamed because of the harshness in which I judge myself. [65-second pause]

RBL: How do you feel?

Paul: I have a strange kind of mixture. I feel loving. I feel sad and I feel good.

RBL: Happy?

Paul: I don't know if it is happy. If I have to go through with this, I can do it. I can survive. At least until I can get a job. And more than likely, I will survive. [Pause] The sadness will be the way I say good-bye, and not because I need so much more therapy. [Pause] But the fact that I cheat myself out of being with you [with tears, sobbing] and with all the people in the group.

RBL: When it finally gets easier.

Paul: [Crying openly] I didn't think of it that way. It's because it is so good.

RBL: That is what I meant, too.

Paul: [14-second silence] It is a hard thing to say, that if I distort myself this way more, I wouldn't be able to enjoy the goodness.

RBL: That's right.

Paul: One piece of candy to enjoy is better than a boxful, if you are too fat.

RBL: [Chuckle, 43-second pause]
       [Large breath of air taken in by Paul]
Paul: I have a terrible headache. . . . I am just wondering now if it is
       because I had to say this today. It may be because I have a bad
       cold also.
RBL: What does "this" refer to? Is it because you consider seriously
       leaving, or because you're loving. Which is the "this"?
Paul: [With a slight chuckle] Even before you said it, I knew it was the
       question that I had to ask myself. It was clear that I knew I had to
       say that I had to seriously consider leaving, but it may well have
       been that if I have to leave, I have to stop clowning around and
       admit that I do love you and respect you. And it is not so much
       that it has to be said, but that I want to say it. [This is all said qui-
       etly, thoughtfully, slowly, with a trembling voice.]
RBL: It has to be said for your integrity.
Paul: Yeah, that's it.
RBL: These are words that the little boy couldn't say, even on an occa-
       sion when, maybe, it was called for.
Paul: Mmm. I don't know, but that is one of the best things that has
       happened to me since I have been here. Whatever happens in my
       life, it is clear, and it is more clear lately, being able to say that, I
       don't know where it comes from. . . . My wife, I know, also
       wants to be clearer on these issues . . . but she can't. [Tears]
RBL: You know that your life is not threatened anymore. You often felt
       that it was. You helped yourself on such occasions, because there
       was no better way, with confusion, but no more. [Pause] You are
       getting away from the horror [pause] which didn't really exist in
       the first place.
Paul: Right, and in my case it was so real. What I have to be a little
       more concerned about now is how much I like you. I know the
       gratifying aspects of distorting myself. This I don't know very
       well yet. It is still philosophic here, I understand . . .
RBL: That is enough for today.

The "abrasive" patient was no more. He had vanished. A loving and
lovable human being appeared in his stead.

Primitive Object-Relations
and Impaired Structuralization
in the Abrasive Patient

Richard Lasky

A woman noticed her little boy kneading something between his hands. She asked him what it was, and he replied, "Shit." Somewhat taken aback, she nonetheless had the presence of mind to ask him what he was making. He said, "a Mommy." She was, quite naturally, very upset by this and she told her husband about it as soon as he came home. When he approached the child he also saw the boy kneading something between his hands. Very distressed, he too asked the child what he was kneading, and his son said, "Shit." When he asked the child what he was making the little boy said, "a Daddy." After careful consideration, they decided to place their son in treatment. Alone with the therapist, in the initial consultation, the boy was kneading something between his hands. The therapist said, "I bet I know what you're kneading between your hands." The boy looked up quizzically and the therapist said, "I bet you've got shit in your hands." The little boy nodded affirmatively. The therapist then went on: "And I bet I know what you're making, too. You're making a Therapist!" The child looked carefully into his hands for a moment and then looked up and said, "Nope. Not enough shit." —Mr. A

Patients who irritate their therapists intentionally, who verbally attack, emotionally assault, happily challenge, psychologically abuse, and cheerfully depreciate their therapists . . . and who may also be generally obnoxious and disagreeable in many, if not all, of their interpersonal relationships . . . are no rare commodity (Bak, 1960). A tendency to behave hatefully; to be nasty, impudent, or sarcastic; and to mistreat others is not restricted to any single diagnostic category (Arlow et al., 1973; Hamburg, 1972; Hartmann, Kris, & Loewenstein, 1945). However, there are some diagnostic categories that lend themselves more readily than do others to abrasive, abusive, and offensive behavior (Kernberg, 1966, 1975, 1976; Kohut, 1964; Lasky, 1979; Rank, 1949; Volkan, 1976).

Richard Lasky, Ph.D., is on the faculties of New York University, the Postgraduate Center for Mental Health, and the College of Physicians and Surgeons of Columbia University in New York City.

In the neuroses, abrasive behavior is not uncommon for patients with sadomasochistic conflicts (Brenner, 1971). Irritating and provocative behavior regularly occurs, within limits, in the intense revival of unresolved oedipal conflicts which appear in the emerging transference neurosis as well (Arlow, 1961). To consider an area of more profound pathology, the character disorders, abrasive and abusive patients frequently suffer *narcissistic* (Kohut, 1962; Lasky, 1979), *borderline* (Lasky, in press-b; Lichtenstein, 1965; Mahler, 1961, 1968), *psychopathic/sociopathic* (Friedlander, 1945), and *passive-aggressive* (Rank, 1949; Reich, 1964; Rubinfine, 1962; Volkan, 1963) character disorders. Such behavior is also common, particularly where one sees the emergence of passive/demanding dependency, oral-sadistic, anal-aggressive, and symbiotic-parasitic features, in the *infantile* character disorder (Brenner, 1970; Jacobson, E., 1946; Lasky, 1979). Extremely abrasive conduct, and worse, sometimes occurs with schizophrenic patients who are unable to exercise control over strong impulses, and who may suffer from an especially low tolerance for frustration or disappointment (Spitz, 1961). Objectionable behavior is also not uncommon during the manic phase of some affectively psychotic individuals (Lasky, 1982; Slap, 1967; Spiegel, 1959, 1966).

This short list, which is in no way even close to being complete, illustrates the wide variety of diagnostic categories in which the clinician may encounter abrasive patients. In the consistently abrasive or abusive patient who usually is rather seriously disturbed, as differentiated from the neurotic patient whose abrasiveness is partially inhibited, sporadic, and usually rather transient in nature, primitive object-relations and impaired structuralization are usually implicated in the ill-treatment afforded the therapist and others. This seems to be true despite the fact that these impediments may lead to a wide variety of clinical syndromes, and will be influential in the development of diverse forms of mental organization. But because abrasive, abusive, unfair, or provocative behavior cannot be said to be centered in a single diagnostic category, or even in a distinct set of closely related diagnostic categories, theorists and psychotherapists work under something of a handicap in the formulation and development of a unified treatment approach.

One may say that, where neurotic patients are concerned, most abrasive or pernicious conduct represents some feature of an infantile conflict to which the patient is fixated (Lasky, 1978, in press-a; Sandler, 1960). It represents a process of displacement in which an apperceptive mass from the patient's past (in which is included prior experiences and in which the traits, characteristics, beliefs, attitudes, opinions, action tendencies, mannerisms, and so forth, of significant others in the patient's past find representation) is recapitulated in the treatment in the form of *the transference neurosis* (Spitz, 1958, 1964, 1965). Arrogance, derision, insolence, surliness, impertinence, unreasonable demandingness, ridicule, scorn, contempt, rudeness, and so forth are usually passing phenomena which arise in the context of those natural regressions that the patient undergoes in the ordinary course of an analysis (Reich, 1960). Neurotic patients suffer most from fixation, and suffer least from primitive object-relations and impaired structuralization, throughout the entire range of mental disorders, by definition. Whether the patient is repeating something exactly the way it happened, or is repeating something in radically altered forms, fixation appears (as a manifestation of the compulsion to repeat) in every transference demand made by the patient on the analyst (Loewald, 1961). Outside the analysis, fixation is represented in the form of symptoms. One may see this illustrated in the following clinical vignette.

Mr. A was an only child, and aside from his parents his only other living relative was his paternal grandmother. With the outbreak of World War II Mr. A's father was drafted into the armed services. He was sent overseas into combat when Mr. A's mother was 2-months pregnant. He did not return home until Mr. A was 5 years old. Mr. A's mother lived with her husband's mother since just prior to giving birth. She dissolved the marriage, however, and left Mr. A with his grandmother when he was 3 years old. Apparently, Mr. A's grandmother criticized Mr. A's mother, constantly and unmercifully, in person and in her letters to her son. His father's letters home to his wife regularly echoed his mother's complaints about her. The nature of the criticisms were often vague and general, but at times consisted of powerfully condemning allegations of her deficiencies and ineptitudes as a mother and often derogated her as a human being in general. This constant carping and hostility toward her was, ostensibly, the reason why she left. It was never clear to Mr. A why she left and did not take him with her. He suspected throughout childhood, and even as an adult, that her leaving was his fault. It was common practice for his father and his grandmother to keep Mr. A confused about things.

Throughout his childhood and adolescence Mr. A was indoctrinated with the idea that his mother simply abandoned him, that she left suddenly and without reason. It was not until he met her as an adult that Mr. A learned of the unrelenting harassment and the campaign of demoralization practiced on her by his father and by his grandmother. Also, throughout his childhood and his adolescence he wondered why his mother never wrote to him, called him on the telephone, or made any other attempts to contact him. His father and grandmother always claimed not to know how to reach her, and used the fact that she never contacted Mr. A as proof of her unworthiness as a mother. As an adult Mr. A found out, with independent substantiation, that his mother had tried to contact him for years: Her letters to Mr. A were intercepted and destroyed by his father and grandmother, her telephone calls were interfered with, and her at-

tempts to physically visit her son were successfully frustrated by his father and grandmother. After years of trying, she did give up; the courts
did not enforce visitation rights for her because she left her son "volun-
tarily" and because she divorced her husband when he was fighting overseas. Mr. A's mother finally moved to another part of the country, remarried, and successfully raised a new family (with three children).

Mr. A called his father, "Father," and he always called his grandmother, "Mother." He routinely referred to them both as his "Parents."
During the time between his mother's leaving and his father's return, Mr.
A's grandmother was not alone; she had a male friend who, in many
ways, served to complete the family triad (despite the fact that he was not
a full-time live-in guest in their home). When Mr. A's father returned,
grandmother's companion was cast aside, and father, son, and grandmother lived together thereafter. From that time until their deaths Mr. A's
father lived with Mr. A's grandmother, and neither was known ever to
have had a subsequent romantic attachment. Mr. A evidently knew a little
about why his mother was gone because he often thought, as a child, that
he would disappear (as did his mother) if he displeased them. Mr. A's
"parents" engaged in critical and intimidating behavior with him. Much
of their aggression toward him was in support of an incestuous glamori-
zation of themselves and their relationship, and their abuse of him when
he questioned their relationship or asked about his mother did much to reinforce his fears.

The complex and interesting permutations of Mr. A's oedipal conflicts, and the direct and indirect incestuous overstimulation evoked in
him by these arrangements, will not be presented further here. Not because of a lack of interest or because they are unimportant, but because of
limitations in space and limitations in the scope of this article. We can,
however, look for a moment at how Mr. A recapitulated the atmosphere
of his childhood in his treatment.

The joke that began this essay was told by Mr. A, and he was the
source of many other explicitly hostile anti-therapist jokes. If he noticed
even a single hair out of place on his therapist he would say, "What did
you comb your hair with this morning, an egg-beater?" He complained
about his analyst's conservative clothing, claiming that his analyst's sub-
dued manner of dressing must reflect a bland and uninteresting personality. At other times he expressed envy of the therapist's appearance, saying that his "starched, snowy-white shirts, restrained suits and ties, and
meticulous grooming" made him seem "immaculate" and consequently,
"both perfect and unreachable." Mr. A regularly alternated between immediate unquestioning agreement with his analyst's comments and disdainful rejection and dismissal of his ideas. Mr. A went through stages
when he told his therapist that he had to lose weight because it was both
unhealthy and extremely ugly. He never missed an opportunity to point

out a contradiction of his therapist's, an error, an inconsistency, or a mistake. Mr. A regularly gave his analyst the benefit of his advice on how to redecorate his office so that it would be both attractive and comfortable. How reminiscent of the way his grandmother and his father redirected their hostility and criticisms onto him when his mother was no longer available! They remained hypercritical with him even into adulthood.

Sometimes Mr. A related to his analyst as if the analyst were one of his "parents." In this transferential repetition, he experienced his therapist as being continuously angry with him and uniformly critical of him. He went through that unique and special dual experience that all neurotic patients inevitably undergo, *each in their own version*, in psychoanalysis; that is, he was acutely aware of an intense feeling and belief that his analyst disliked him, and he harbored an almost unshakable conviction that his therapist viewed him with a jaundiced eye, while simultaneously knowing, at least intellectually, that this was not true. In subordination to the repetition compulsion Mr. A was often insulting, contemptuous, critical, obnoxious, passive-aggressive, and abrasive in a number of other ways. He was trying to draw out of his analyst, in reality, the harshly critical attitudes of his "parents" through constant attack and irritation. His provocations were also engineered to gratify certain sadomasochistic transformations he developed in response to the critical and harsh attitudes of his so-called "parents." In the further service of those sadomasochistic tendencies (and as a defense in other ways, such as in the transformation of having been a passive victim into becoming an active perpetrator, in an identification with the aggressors) he often reversed roles, treating his analyst as if the analyst were he and then acting cruelly toward the therapist as if he, Mr. A, were now his "parents." Another transference manifestation that emerged in the analysis was Mr. A's fear that his analyst would abandon him, as his mother did (or so he believed), if he were not perfect ("immaculate"). It was Mr. A's underlying and unquestioned belief, even when only unconscious, that his mother left him because of something bad about him, or because of bad things that he did but could not remember doing, and not because she was irresponsible as his "parents" claimed. He thought they were telling him the truth, but were bending it a little to shield him from self-knowledge of his badness and fault in her leaving. Mr. A's belief was reinforced by the constant criticism directed at him. In this version of the transference much of his abrasive conduct in treatment was a manifestation of this, as he tried out with his therapist all the awful ways he imagined he behaved with his mother to cause her to leave. And this alternated with being very good, pleasing, obsequious, servile, fawning, and so forth, in order not to lose the analyst. Finally, his greatest challenge to his therapist and his fondest and most satisfying threat, when feeling critical of his analyst, was to menace his therapist with leaving treatment prematurely.

Mr. A was diagnostically neurotic, and like most neurotics, the abrasive qualities he demonstrated in therapy were often symbolic, rarely overtly destructive, generally confined to verbal expression rather than gross behavioral acting-out, and experienced simultaneously as both legitimate and ego-dystonic. The abrasiveness of the neurotic is more like the slow chipping away of a chronic erosion than it is like an avalanche. The abrasiveness of patients who have disorders of more than neurotic severity is usually more extreme, more florid, less manageable, and not often seen by the patient himself or herself as a symptom of conflict. The hard-earned ego attributes, the well-structured superego, and the intact object-relations (object constancy, object consistency, and sufficient introjective identifications) of the neurotic keeps abrasive conduct under control so that the neurotic patient does not usually overstep the limits generally considered acceptable in a therapy relationship (Novey, 1955). Any patient may fondly dream of punching his or her therapist right in the nose, but one would not normally dream of doing so in reality (Angel, 1971). At least, not if one is merely neurotic. A less-controlled abrasiveness of the kind that may actually get out of hand—that which spills over into what we usually think of as a *psychotic* or *delusional transference* (that is, a transference relationship that has regressed to the point where the patient is entirely unable to use observing-ego attributes and other executive-ego functions)—is considerably more common among persons suffering from a psychosis or from a character disorder, than with neurotics. It may readily be seen, in extreme and unrepentant form for example, as an act that is sometimes intentional and sometimes unintentional, in patients who suffer from the narcissistic character disorder. Let us single out the narcissistic character disorder for a closer look, as it is perhaps one of the best examples of a diagnostic category in which abrasiveness is the rule.

In a discussion of narcissistic difficulties one wishes to differentiate between persons who have suffered a *narcissistic injury*, of whatever magnitude, and persons who suffer from a *narcissistic character disorder* (Brodey, 1965; Freud, S., 1914; Panel Report, 1962, 1969, 1973; Pulver, 1970). Everyone is subject to narcissistic injury, on a regular basis, throughout life. Reactions to narcissistic trauma may range on the one hand from mild virtually nonexistent reverberations, to major pathological dysfunction on the other. In most people the most benign form of narcissistic insult, because it is unconscious and because it affects a nonpredominating area of mental functioning in healthy adults, is that which defies omnipotent archaic self-representations, that is, those self-representations which are merged with omnipotent parental representations, which are stored unchanged from their original development in earliest childhood, which are stored in the deepest recesses of the unconscious, and which operate only minimally in generally healthy adult mental functioning. This remains true despite the fact that in the realm of primary-process operations every disappointment, frustration, delay in gratification, and rejection—no matter how small, unrealistic, or inconsequential—challenges infantile and ingrained primitive omnipotence (Freud, S., 1914). In relatively healthy individuals, including neurotics, sovereignty of ego functioning and maturity of superego functioning keeps such tiny rents in the fabric of narcissism from becoming disproportionately influential or disorganizing (Freeman, 1964). At their very worst these small injuries make some mark, but even so they usually are reflected in relatively (or proportionately) small oscillations in ego and superego functioning; they influence comparably small fluctuations in the regulation of self-esteem; and they are usually rather transient. At best, which is usually the case in healthy adults, they are subjectively and objectively unobservable and frequently even undiscernible (Reich, 1960).

Where major, rather than minor, assaults of self-esteem and disruption of narcissistic integrity occur (as in the loss of a loved one through separation or death; the loss of a limb, an eye, or other body-part; being subjected to a major illness such as a severe heart attack or a stroke; failure in business, social, or educational strivings; or in economic disaster or natural disasters, and so forth) relatively healthy individuals—which context once again includes neurotics—usually show clear and unmistakable signs of narcissistic pathology. This seems to be true across the board among more disturbed patients too, no matter which diagnostic category seems to suit them best. Even though narcissistic trauma and their sequelae are usually expressed in a manner specific to the main diagnostic category the patient falls into, it is nonetheless in this situation that the mistake of diagnosis is most commonly made. Not infrequently, the self-absorption displayed by someone in response to a severe narcissistic injury, or the regressive demands made by a patient overwhelmed by a narcissistic wound, is misunderstood and consequently may be treated as if it is the more profound pathology one encounters in the narcissistic character disorder. Self-absorbed, seemingly selfish, narcissistically regressed patients often present difficulties for the therapist because they can at times really be quite unpleasant, but one must understand that the role and the meaning of abrasiveness and offending conduct is not identical in these patients and in patients with a narcissistic character disorder. The problem, in addition to sloppy diagnostics, is that they frequently appear, at least superficially, to resemble one another.

In considering the special dynamics of the narcissistic character disorder that may provide a look at the roots of abrasiveness, one must note that the early childhood environment of such patients is characteristically deficient in the supply and maintenance of libidinal resources (Jacobson, 1946; Lewin, 1954; Lichtenstein, 1964). In the general process of development infants are initially conflicted over extending object-love because, from an economic point of view, whatever libidinal cathexis they direct to an object results in an equivalent depletion of self-directed libido (Freud, S., 1914). If one recalls that the psychoanalytic model is based on a closed hydraulic system, one then can see that object-cathexis inevitably leads to an equal lowering of narcissistic-cathexis. In the development of object-love, where libidinal cathexis is withdrawn from the self and directed at an object, loving is experienced as a loss (or as a depletion) whereas being loved, where libidinal cathexis is directed to the self, is experienced as a narcissistic enhancement. The child's initial ability to experience being loved is very mechanistic, and is measured strictly by the extent to which object-libidinal strivings are gratified. That is, the child learns to love the mother who feeds him or her (satisfying the object-libidinal striving involved in being hungry) and remains indifferent to the woman who bore him or her if she is uninvolved in taking care of his or her needs on a regular basis in a consistent way (which gratifies no object-libidinal strivings). Since the child's ego is not yet at the point where he or she can make meaningful cause-and-effect connections between the subtleties of social interaction, he or she is in the position of extending unconflicted object-libido to the mother who feeds, while simultaneously resisting this because of the cost involved in the diminishment of narcissistic-libido which the child does not connect properly with the first part of this operation. The solution is identification (Kohut, 1966).

In oral incorporative identification, the child "merges" with the object so that there is effectively, from his or her limited point of view, no difference between self and the object (the first differentiations between awareness of the self and a different awareness of the world of objects cannot be examined here because of limitations in space and scope). If the child incorporates the object (person or her representation) so that they subjectively exist as a single unit, then it is not possible any longer to lose self-directed libidinal cathexis by diverting, from self to object, one's libidinal investments. This dual-cathexis (Freud, A., 1952) in which we see a uniting of object-libido and narcissistic-libido, is what differentiates object-attention and object-love. Object-attention only is extended to successfully exploit the environment. This type of investment truly treats the satisfying person as if she were merely an inanimate object that exists solely to gratify whatever object-libidinal striving is paramount at the moment for the child. People are like things to be used for what they have to offer, in much the same way that one squeezes juice out of an orange and throws the rind away.

When the environment is not generally gratifying, as postulated earlier, the child cannot take the next step in identification and replace object-attention with object-love. If the environment is sufficiently depriving the child will die, or become psychotic. In the case of the character disorders, and in the case of the narcissistic character disorder specifically, the level of frustration, deprivation, and disappointment in early infancy is usually just below the level deemed adequate for proper development, but not so deficient as to cause psychosis or death. This model is, by the way, not in competition with other, including organic, models of psychosis; this merely describes one contribution to a many-faceted process (Jacobson, 1964). The achievement of object-love is what changes people in the child's environment from things and objects into humans, for in object-love the child will protect loved objects from harm as he or she would protect himself or herself. Differences in the nature and amount of deficiency in the childhood environment account for the various kinds of character disorders, just as the same kind of variability, but to a lesser extent, accounts for the degree of severity in any given character disorder. Additional issues in early childhood development also play a role in the exploitive and often sadistic behaviors of patients with a narcissistic character disorder, such as the inability to tolerate the depressive struggles that attend object loss (if they are in the healthier end of the spectrum, and have been able to identify minimally with someone in their environment) (Kernberg, 1969). In this case, much of their aggressiveness (for them, abrasiveness would be a vast improvement) is specifically designed to prevent the development of object-love by swamping the relationship with aggression in order to avoid the inevitable, as they see it, loss of the object in the future. From their perspective, not consciously of course, what they invest in the person through extending object-love will be lost when the person inevitably frustrates and disappoints them, and they believe that they will be better off if they don't make the investment to begin with; their experience is that the "object" absconds with some of their libido, like a thief in the night, leaving them with less than they had before they began. And that hurts. And, therefore, one is legitimately entitled to direct aggression at anyone who poses the threat, by virtue of their being a tempting love object, and who will by definition hurt them badly, even if they have not done it yet. After all, it feels to them, it's just a matter of time. This occurs because the primary model of mothering took that shape in reality. Mother was there for them just enough to get them involved, and then frustrated and disappointed them after they were "hooked."

We now have three converging approaches for understanding hostile, abrasive, and even abusive behavior in patients with a narcissistic character disorder: (a) thoughtlessness because the patient cannot identify with the needs and rights of the therapist; (b) rage in response to frustration and disappointment, which is uncontrolled by the need to protect a love-object (the therapist) from harm; and (c) aggression directed at the therapist to ward off the possibility of dangerous and inevitably painful identification. The foregoing has been a description that has implicitly included the idea that there are impairments in ego functioning and in the operation of the superego that evolve in the production of such disordered object-relations. Before making them more explicit, some brief clinical examples can serve to illustrate how these three types of influences operate in therapy.

Type A: On a day in midwinter, with slush and rock-salt covering her boots, Ms. B rushed into her therapist's office *through the lightest part of his rug* and threw herself, boots and all, onto his couch. She took a few deep breaths and then sat up abruptly to pull off her boots, splattering his wall in the process. She dumped her boots onto the rug, one on a dark portion and one on a light. She then noticed that the bottom of the couch was wet so she picked up a hand-knitted afghan blanket from a nearby chair which she then placed on the wet part of the couch so that her feet would not be damp. Ms. B was not angry with her therapist. She had something important to her on her mind and just was not attentive to all the rest of what was going on. She was not the kind of person who would choose to harm her therapist intentionally, but she was also not the kind of person who would not do it intentionally.

Mr. C, on arising from a chair, accidentally hooked something he had in a pocket on the leather seat and tore it. In his next session he and his therapist were unable to determine whether this was purely an accident, or if it was the unconscious expression of some anger. The analyst suggested that they examine in detail exactly what took place physically, to tear the cushion, in order to prevent any future repetitions (even if it was purely an accident). Mr. C thought his therapist was crazy to spend so much time trying to figure out how this had happened. According to him the analyst should just have chalked it up to office overhead. He mentioned in passing that if he had repeatedly torn the chair, he could understand why his therapist would want to take special precautions against it happening again. Mr. C summed up the situation by wondering whether his therapist was just the kind of person who cared more about furniture than people.

Type B: Ms. D entered into a therapy arrangement where she would be obligated to pay for every scheduled session whether she showed up for it or not, a fairly customary arrangement, although certainly not the only one practiced by New York City analysts. After some time she informed her analyst that she would like to take riding lessons more frequently (she was from a wealthy family, owned her own horse which was kept at a stable in the city, and already was taking two lessons per week), and she further informed him that she had made arrangements to use the time from one of their regularly scheduled sessions *on an every-other-week basis* for riding, which she did. She was told at that time that she would have to pay for those sessions if she wanted the time held for her, as her therapist was unwilling to set time aside on an every-other-week basis (she had three sessions per week regularly scheduled). Ms. D was furious with him and took the position that unless he could prove to her satisfaction that he had turned away a patient for that time (every other week) and therefore could prove a loss of income, that she had no intention of paying him. Note carefully that she told him this not at the time that he informed her, when she could have stated her objections, but after she had used a month of services in this way, and when it could only have been solved (by his changing his mind or by her choosing to cancel her third session entirely) in retrospect. She felt no embarrassment or discomfort about refusing to pay him, and seemed entirely unable to appreciate the problem inherent in not living up to their previous agreement. In fact, if anything, she felt that he was exploiting her and trying to cheat her, and before she left treatment, in a rage, told him in great detail how this issue made his "Jewishness" very apparent to all and sundry. She never did pay him for *any* of the sessions of that month.

Type C: Mr. E was a student in a related mental health profession, who came to treatment recommended by a close friend of his. This friend worked as a counselor in a mental health center where Mr. E's eventual therapist was his supervisor. Mr. E came to treatment specifically requesting psychoanalysis which he hoped to be able to use as a training analysis for a psychoanalytic institute he wanted to attend the following year. From the very first treatment hour Mr. E was verbally abusive. Interestingly, this was not true of three exploratory consultation sessions that occurred before Mr. E and his therapist made arrangements to work together. If his therapist said something he did not agree with Mr. E would tell him not to be such a "stupid ass-hole." If his therapist interrupted to ask a clarifying question, Mr. E wanted to know if he was a "fucking moron who couldn't even follow the thread of a simply story." When his therapist made a mistake, he was a "scumbag." These examples were merely the tip of the iceberg, but will have to suffice for now. After not too long a time Mr. E's analyst spoke with him about this and Mr. E was indignant. He thought his therapist was a "piece of shit" for trying to tell him that he was not entitled to say whatever came to mind. When his therapist mentioned that the problem was not with Mr E saying everything that came to mind, but was with the fact that this was the only thing that came to mind, Mr. E was furious. When it was pointed out to Mr. E that he was not supposed to be complacent about the fact that he was so abusive, and that he was inappropriate in having so little conflict about it, he escalated his abusiveness by contacting other therapists in the area (including the person who referred him) to inform them of his therapist's "bizarre inability to handle free association." No amount of discussion about the difference between coming to therapy for transference resolution versus coming to therapy for transference gratification was of any help. Nor was any transference interpretation of any value. His stock reply to every therapeutic attempt was, "So what, Fuck-face?" Convinced that the problem was his therapist's, and thirsting for revenge because his therapist was "trying to inhibit [his] freedom of expression," Mr. E terminated the treatment. He then undertook a slander campaign against the analyst in the professional community. (Because of the limitations in scope and space, some other paper will have to deal with the topics of how one copes with such behavior when one is the victim of such a patient, and how one copes with one's own feelings while undergoing it (Oremland & Windholz, 1971).

No matter which character disorder a patient falls into it will usually be true that the object-relations of abrasive patients specifically will always have in common the quality of primitivity just described. And this will be true even if they are aligned somewhat differently, as long as the magnitude of their pathology is sufficient to place them within the diagnostic category of the character disorders. One may speculate as well, regarding fluctuations in ego functioning, that neurotic victimizing patients may resemble those with the narcissistic character disorder in the following way: It may be the case that *all* patients who treat their therapists as if they were objects, in the true sense of the word, instead of people, may have (no matter what their diagnosis) regressed to the level of functioning just described as the *standard* for the narcissistic character disorder during the period of time they have lost their normally restraining empathy for the object of their aggression (the therapist). In other words, the primitive stage in which the patient with a narcissistic character disorder is arrested (or retarded, one might say) is qualitatively as accessible to the neurotic who moves in and out of it, depending on regression and fluctuations in ego functioning and environmental pressures. What is normal for the narcissistic character disorder is unusual for the neurotic, but by no means impossible. And this throws some light on why merely neurotic patients can behave so horribly at times.

As a further consideration of impairment in psychic structuralization leading to brutalizations of the therapist, one may wish to consider the not uncommon fact that the identifications of emotionally assaultive patients are sometimes overtly aggressive in nature and content (Kron, 1971). There is no reason why such identifications must necessarily be tempered by mergers (or simultaneous identifications) with loving or benign self- and object-representations, particularly when they reflect or are otherwise involved in conflict. And when such identifications are embroiled in conflict, the likelihood is greater than not that the moderating influences of the ego, and the restraints demanded by other aspects (beyond these particular identifications) of the superego, will be reduced in effectiveness leaving unneutralized the sadism that then gets directed at the therapist (Kohut, 1968). If the ego cannot inhibit or transform abusive inclinations, the impairment is obvious. Concerning the superego, one will recall that it acts as a reservoir for almost all the identifications, that identifications serve as the most important and numerous of the superego's contents, and that identifications in the form of aspirations make up the sum total of the ego-ideal. Concrete identifications with genuinely pathological characters who are in actuality aggravating, disdainful, hostile, contemptuous, vulgar, and unpleasant, and similarly pathological *aspirations* in the ego-ideal, represent another flaw in superego structuralization common in abusive or abrasive patients; identifications with criminals, thugs, sadists, and so forth is not limited or defined by diagnostic categories (Murray, 1964).

In a final remark on impairment of psychic structuralization, pathology in the ego-ideal, as described above, leads to disruption of the way in which the ego-ideal serves a bridging function between the ego and the rest of the superego (Hendrick, 1964). In neurotic patients resources usually exist which can combat a snowballing effect which has pathology ever increasing in these intersystemic relationships except when they are subjected to unique stresses (of an internal nature or from the environment, or both), and in this way they are characteristically different from patients with higher-order pathologies.

As mentioned earlier, the fact that unwelcome conduct is not organized along the lines of diagnostic categories hampers an attempt to suggest a unified therapeutic approach. However on a case by case, or group by group, basis some obvious tactics suggest themselves. For example, one would expect abrasive behavior in a patient with a narcissistic character disorder to be reduced in proportion to the successful development of frustration tolerance. Or with a schizophrenic patient, enhancements of reality-testing and the strengthening of other secondary-process functioning would lead to less objectionable behavior. Obvious limitations prevent a category by category examination of all the other diagnostic groups, and how one achieves the above-mentioned, and other, goals therapeutically will not be discussed here since this is not a technique paper. However, the important point is that the abrasive patient usually cannot be controlled simply by imposing rules from without. The real cure will come from understanding the individual's dynamics, and then promoting structuralization, autonomy, and maturity from within.

REFERENCES

Angel, K. (1971). Unanalyzability and narcissistic transference. *Psychoanalytic Quarterly, 40,* 264–276.

Arlow, J. (1961). Conflict, regression, and symptom formation. *Journal of the American Psychoanalytical Association, 9,* 12–22.

Arlow, J., et al. (1973). The role of aggression in human adaptation. *Psychoanalytic Quarterly, 42,* 178–184.

Bak, R. (1960). Aggression and symptom formation. *Journal of the American Psychoanalytic Association, 9,* 9–27.

Brenner, C. (1970). Problems in the psychoanalytic theory of aggression. *Psychoanalytic Quarterly, 39*, 121–137.

Brenner, C. (1971). The psychoanalytic theory of aggression. *International Journal of Psycho-Analysis, 52*, 137–144.

Brodey, W. M. (1965). The dynamics of narcissism. *The Psychoanalytic Study of the Child, 20*, 165–193.

Freeman, T. (1964). Some aspects of pathological narcissism. *Journal of the American Psychoanalytic Association, 12*, 9–23.

Freud, A. (1952). Aggression in relation to emotional development: Normal and pathological. In *Writings of Anna Freud*. New York: International Universities Press.

Freud, S. (1914). On narcissism. In J. Strachey et al. (Eds.), *Standard edition of the writings of Sigmund Freud*. London: Hogarth Press.

Friedlander, K. (1945). Formation of the anti-social character. *The Psychoanalytic Study of the Child, 1*, 189–203.

Hamburg, D. (1972). A developmental approach to human aggression. *Psychoanalytic Quarterly, 43*, 185–196.

Hartmann, H., Kris, E., & Loewenstein, R. (1945). Notes on the theory of aggression. *The Psychoanalytic Study of the Child, 1*, 9–36.

Hendrick, I. (1964). Narcissism and the pre-puberty ego ideal. *Journal of the American Psychoanalytic Association, 12*, 522–528.

Jacobson, E. (1946). The effect of disappointment on ego and superego development. *The Psychoanalytic Review, 53*, 129–147.

Jacobson, E. (1964). *The self and the object world*. New York: International Universities Press.

Kernberg, O. (1966). Structural derivatives of object relations. *International Journal of Psychoanalysis, 47*, 236–253.

Kernberg, O. (1969). Factors in the psychoanalytic treatment of narcissistic personalities. *Bulletin of the Menninger Clinic, 33*, 191–196.

Kernberg, O. (1975). *Borderline conditions and pathological narcissism*. New York: Jacob Aronson.

Kohut, H. (1962). Thoughts on narcissism and narcissistic rage. *The Psychoanalytic Study of the Child, 27*, 360–400.

Kohut, H. (1966). Forms and transformations of narcissism. *Journal of the American Psychoanalytic Association, 14*, 636–653.

Kohut, H. (1964). *Analysis of the self*. New York: International Universities Press.

Kohut, H. (1968). The psychoanalytic treatment of the narcissistic personality. *The Psychoanalytic Study of the Child, 23*, 86–113.

Kron, S. R. (1971). Psychoanalytic complications of a narcissistic transference. *Journal of the American Psychoanalytic Association, 19*, 636–653.

Lasky, R. (1978). The impact of object-relations theory on psychoanalytic theory and practice. In H. Greyson & C. Loew (Eds.), *Changing perspectives in psychotherapy*. New York: Spectrum/John Wiley.

Lasky, R. (1979a). Kernberg and Kohut; Treatment of the narcissistic character disorder. *Colloquium, 2*, 35–38.

Lasky, R. (1979b). Archaic, immature, and infantile personality characteristics. In L. Saretsky et al. (Eds.), *Integrating ego psychology and object-relations theory: Psychoanalytic perspectives on psychopathology*. Dubuque, IA: Kendall/Hunt.

Lasky, R. (1982). *Evaluating criminal responsibility in multiple personality and the related dissociative disorders: A psychoanalytic consideration*. Springfield, IL: Charles C Thomas.

Lasky, R. (in press-a). Dynamics and treatment of the "oedipal winner." *The Psychoanalytic Review*.

Lasky, R. (in press-b). *Key concepts in psychoanalytic theory and practice*. New York: Jacob Aronson.

Lewin, B. (1954). Sleep, narcissistic neurosis, and the psychoanalytic situation. *Psychoanalytic Quarterly, 23*, 487–510.

Lichtenstein, H. (1964). The role of narcissism in the emergence and maintenance of a primary identification. *International Journal of Psychoanalysis, 45*, 49–56.

Lichtenstein, H. (1965). Toward a metapsychological definition of the concept of self. *International Journal of Psychoanalysis, 45*, 117–128.

Loewald, H. (1961). On the therapeutic action of psychoanalysis. *International Journal of Psychoanalysis, 40*, 16–33.

Mahler, M. (1961). Sadness and grief in infancy and childhood: Loss and restoration of the symbiotic love object. *The Psychoanalytic Study of the Child, 16,* 332–351.

Mahler, M., et al. (1968). *On human symbiosis and the vicissitudes of individuation.* New York: International Universities Press.

Murray, J. M. (1964). Narcissism and the ego-ideal. *Journal of the American Psychoanalytic Association, 12,* 477–511.

Novey, S. (1955). The role of the superego and ego-ideal in character formation. *International Journal of Psychoanalysis, 36,* 254–259.

Oremland, J.D., & Windholz, E. (1971). Some specific transference, countertransference, and supervisory problems in the analysis of a narcissistic personality. *International Journal of Psychoanalysis, 52,* 267–275.

Panel Report. (1962). Narcissism. *Journal of the American Psychoanalytic Association, 10,* 593–605.

Panel Report. (1969). Narcissistic resistance. *Journal of the American Psychoanalytic Association, 17,* 7–115.

Panel Report. (1973). Narcissism. *Journal of the American Psychoanalytic Association, 21,* 34–69.

Rank, B. (1949). Aggression. *The Psychoanalytic Study of the Child, 3/4,* 43–48.

Reich. A. (1960). Pathological forms of self-esteem regulation. *The Psychoanalytic Study of the Child, 15,* 215–232.

Reich, A. (1964). Early identifications as archaic elements in the superego. *Journal of the American Psychoanalytic Association, 2,* 218–238.

Rubinfine, F. (1962). Maternal stimulation, psychic structure, and early object relations. *The Psychoanalytic Study of the Child, 17,* 265–282.

Sandler, J. (1960). On the concept of the superego. *The Psychoanalytic Study of the Child, 15,* 128–162.

Slap, J. (1967). Freud's views on pleasure and aggression. *Journal of the American Psychoanalytic Association, 15,* 370–375.

Spiegel, L. A. (1959). The self, the sense of self, and perception. *The Psychoanalytic Study of the Child, 14,* 81–109.

Spiegel, L. A. (1966). Affects in relation to self and object. *The Psychoanalytic Study of the Child, 21,* 69–92.

Spitz, R. A. (1958). On the genesis of superego components. *The Psychoanalytic Study of the Child, 13,* 375–404.

Spitz, R. A. (1961). Some early prototypes of ego defenses. *Journal of the American Psychoanalytic Association, 9,* 229–240.

Spitz, R. A. (1964). The derailment of dialogue. *Journal of the American Psychoanalytic Association, 12,* 752–775.

Sptiz, R. A. (1965). *The first year of life.* New York: International Universities Press.

Volkan, V. D. (1963). Transitional fantasies in the analysis of a narcissistic personality. *Journal of the American Psychoanalytic Association, 21,* 352–376.

Volkan, V. D. (1976). *Primitive internalized object-relations.* New York: International Universities Press.

A Session with Jack:
A Demonstration of Mirroring
by Ego-Syntonic Joining

Arnold Bernstein

Several years ago, a group of colleagues* and I began meeting together regularly to exchange views about the theory and practice of psychoanalytic psychotherapy. Our discussions revolved mainly around the various innovative and experimental techniques that we had been utilizing in our practices to resolve resistances and to overcome therapeutic stalemates. We wanted to share information about these procedures, assess their utility, receive feedback, and perhaps formulate a theoretical rationale for their use. Upon the suggestion of the late Professor Benjamin Nelson, who was the nonpractitioner member of our colloquium, we eventually began calling ourselves the Paradigmatic Behaviors Study Seminar.

It was our usual practice to listen to a tape recording of a single therapy session presented by one of the group members and to study and micro-analyze the therapeutic interactions displayed in that session with special attention to the rationale for the therapist's interventions. My experience in that study group also emboldened me to try out new and innovative interventions and to share the results with my colleagues. I found this practice so helpful that I still tape-record and study therapy sessions that I conduct.

Continuing in this tradition, I am venturing to publish verbatim an annotated single therapeutic session in which I undertook what would then have been described as "heroic" measures to resolve a long-standing stalemate in an obstinate case. This report is not of a completed case in which the outline of a successful analysis is portrayed, nor is it a demonstration of a "cure" (except in the very limited sense that resistances can be "cured"); rather it is a presentation limited to a single session in which

Arnold Bernstein, Ph.D., received his doctorate in clinical psychology from Columbia University in 1952. He is a psychoanalyst in private practice in New York City, Professor Emeritus in Psychology at Queens College of the City University of New York, and Dean of Professional Programs at the Center for Modern Psychoanalytic Studies.

*Arthur Blatt, Robert DeNeergaard, Marie Coleman Nelson, Benjamin Nelson, Murray H. Sherman, and Herbert S. Strean.

particular resistances are successfully resolved by the application of particular strategies.

My purpose, in providing an annotated verbatim report of a therapy session in which I mirror a patient's resistances, is to make available to colleagues actual clinical material that they can study in much the same way that surgeons view and study a surgical operation in which some new procedure is being demonstrated, except only that the operative interventions to be observed are verbal and the effects to be studied are psychological. Moreover, since my intent in providing actual clinical material is for the light it casts on problems relating to practice and technique rather than on theory, issues relating to theory, etiology, and diagnosis will only be addressed minimally (Bernstein, 1965).

At the time that our paradigmatic group was holding its meetings, I was treating a man in his middle 50s, whom I shall refer to as Jack, who displayed a particularly refractory and abrasive form of resistance in the context of an intense negative transference. Jack had risen through the ranks from a steelworker to become an executive and, though he was quite sophisticated, street language still came naturally to him. His sessions were never free of the coarsest profanity and obscenity delivered mainly in the form of scatological and anal expletives. From our very first visit Jack assumed a very negative and hostile stance toward me which persisted over the span of years that preceded the session which will comprise the subject of this paper. In this respect the case was somewhat unusual in that persons so negatively inclined toward their analysts did not ordinarily remain with them very long. It has only been in recent years that successful utilization and therapeutic management of negative transferences have been systematically applied within the framework of modern psychoanalysis (Spotnitz, 1969; Spotnitz & Meadow, 1976).

As I am generally quite kind and accepting in my approach to new patients, this derogatory attitude on Jack's part, as will be clear from a reading of the transcript below, was rather patently a manifestation of transference. The negative feelings he displayed toward me were clearly displaced from his deceased father who had been a sergeant in the Polish army and who had been very brutal and frightening to him as well as to his mother. In Jack's words, "The old man scared the shit out of me."

His rage and hatred for "the old man" knew no bounds and they figured prominently in Jack's obsessive ruminations. Jack reported that he broke off verbal contact with his father at age 19 and stopped speaking to him. He finally left home at the age of 32 after 12 years of silence and never saw his father again. This angry spiteful withholding attitude was reenacted in exquisite detail in the treatment and became a prominent feature of his resistance.

In spite of the fact that for years I maintained a consistently accepting, noncritical, and nonjudgmental attitude toward him and listened patiently, Jack frequently accused me of being "just like the old man." "He was fulla crap too!" he said. "I just don't want to cooperate with you," he gratuitously remarked. "You want me to talk. Well, I won't talk!" On another occasion he expostulated, "I'm not giving anybody any satisfaction! —Goddam you—you fuckin' bastard!"

Jack frequently expressed regret that he had ever begun therapy with me, especially because I was Jewish, and he repeatedly made invidious comparisons between me and his former therapist, often voicing the wish that he were still in treatment with him. He once remarked that his old analyst "was clean." Evidently I was more like his family whom he often described in such terms as, "They were a filthy bunch of bastards—smelly and dirty and full of crap!"

Nevertheless, Jack complied with the minimum requirements of treatment. He was punctual, attended regularly, paid on time, lay on the couch, and talked. Beyond that he was fiercely withholding and verbally abusive. In a moment of candor, referring to the analysis, he once confessed, "I don't believe in all of this crap!" He then went on to say, "*Everything* is shit, piss, and corruption."

Instead of talking to me directly or contacting me, he initiated the practice of lying on the couch and "free associating" as if I were not present. He would think out loud, as if to himself, through clenched teeth in a low almost inaudible tone. Sometimes his voice sounded like an angry growl, at other times like a sullen child's. Sometimes he would force out his words explosively accompanied by grunts and sounds and body movements, much as a constipated person might struggle to effect a bowel movement. Characteristically, he would dismiss any verbal contacts by me with a disdainful wave of his hand and a comment like "Fuck you!" or, more often, "You're fulla shit!"

Interpretations proved useless because he himself had already perfected them as an intellectual defense. He would discuss himself as if he were a case history and utilize psychoanalytic jargon and highly schematic reconstructions of his life history to effectively neutralize any emotional impact his communications might have. Until the session I am about to report, nothing I said seemed to penetrate this narcissistic communication barrier.

One of the treatment strategies that had been under study by our group was what Marie Coleman Nelson (Coleman, 1956) had identified as externalization of the toxic introject. But it was not until Murray Sherman, another member of our group, played a recording of a session in which he had employed a very provocative and unusual procedure, which he later described at length under the title, "Play-Fantasy and Gratification in Psychotherapy" (Sherman, 1968), that I was inspired to formulate and apply these new treatment strategies in Jack's case.

After years of "analytic neutrality" and of being a "blank screen," I had not succeeded in diminishing the power of Jack's toxic paternal introject, his self-hatred, anger, nor his feeling of isolation. Nor had I succeeded in dissolving his negative narcissistic transference. Inspired by Sherman's courage and originality, I decided that I would mirror Jack's anal-sadistic defense and become like him. I would act toward him as he had been acting toward me and incidentally the way his father had acted toward him. I would also give Jack carefully titrated doses of his own medicine to stimulate a sort of psychic toxoid response (Spotnitz, 1963) that would immunize his ego from the internal source of self-attack. I arrived at the felicitous idea of responding to everything that Jack said in the next session with an anal-sadistic remark like, "Shit!", "You're full of shit!", "Bullshit!", or variations of the same. What follows is a transcript of what transpired during that session. The strategy proved to be singularly successful in evoking the first major emotional breakthrough in the treatment.

* * *

Jack enters the office and settles on the couch.

P1:   I was having a fantasy out there. [In the waiting room]

T1:   What was your fantasy?

P2:   My fantasy was about the group and Mary [a member of the group]—and it appears she said something—and I said, "Well, according to Freud, page so and so, chapter so and so, he said such and such a thing."—and she got very angry at me—and [he chuckles, enjoying his sadism] I thought it was very funny, as if I was trying to get her angry. She was enjoying the process. Reminds me of last night. I went out with this girl, Therese, and I feel like it's the same thing: [Starts rambling] I'm torn between a desire in a sense, to have her sexually and all of the old stuff comes up, you know. [Starts analyzing] I don't know what the hell it is—whether I like women or not. I guess I do because—I still think it's because of certain guilt feelings I have when I have sex relations with a woman—as if I'm, in a sense, duty bound or something—to be nice to her—to see her more—to tell her I love her and all that sort of business . . .

T2:   [Mirroring interpretation] All that shit.

P3:   Call it shit. Call it anything. [Trying to be reasonable] It *is* shit, because it does interfere with the natural functioning of the individual. Seems artificial—starting all that shit again. It *is* all shit when you come to consider it.

T3:   [Mirroring him] Everything's shit.

P4:   [Pause] Certainly! Why does a person have to undergo all these fuckin' conflicts—in the sense that you can't act spontaneously—without, in a sense, having a sort of subconscious measuring rod as to whether you're acting right or wrong? [Pause. Continues intellectualizing] Reminds me of a guy that opposed my policies once. I got angry with the guy when I really shouldn't have gotten angry. And no doubt part of my apparatus is to get angry with a person instead of taking my time and finding out why they act in such and such a manner and what makes them act that way. [Growls] It's just not my makeup! I guess I'll eventually come around to it. In that sense I'm like my father who had to get angry and oppose you.

P4: [Emphatically] He was full of shit.

T5: [Sighs. Still trying to be reasonable] Well it means that he was full of shit because he didn't know what was motivating him. That's true. [Suddenly belligerent] What are you driving at! [Resistant] I don't know what you're driving at. I don't know what the hell you're driving at! [Mutters to himself] Full of shit! Full of shit! Full of shit! [Then pensively] Full of shit. [Intellectualizing again] What I think is that there's a background formula in my makeup that things *are* full of shit.

T5 [Mirroring] Everything is shit.

P6: Everything is shit. [Mischievously] Does that mean everything is love? [Pause] Everything is shit. [Silence. Quietly] It makes me think I used to shit because I was forced to. [Pause] Everything is shit. My mother and . . .

T6: [Interrupting] Filthy shitty woman! All those women were covered with shit. [Mirroring a communication from a previous session]

P7: All those women—all my aunts confused me. [He was the only child in a household of women]

T7: [Trying to keep him emotionally engaged] They were all covered with shit! [i.e., They were dirty]

P8: They weren't covered with shit. I just couldn't understand them. They confused me.

T8: They were dirty. [This is deliberately ambiguous, reflecting his confusion between sex and excreta]

P9: They were dirty sexually. [Pause] Dirt and sex go hand in hand, I guess. [13-second pause] I didn't understand them, I guess.

T9: [Mirroring] You're an ignorant bastard.

P10: [Belligerently] Who's an ignorant bastard?

T10: You. You're an ignorant bastard.

P11: [Joining me] So I'm an ignorant bastard.

T11: [Provocatively] And you're full of shit besides.

P12: [Laughs appreciatively. He has fully recovered his equanimity. Changes the subject] I was just thinking about that job I unloaded on my friend, Joe.

T12: [Increasing the pressure] You unloaded shit on your friend Joe!

P13: [Ignoring my provocation] It wasn't shit. It was just a job I could have done better.

T13: [Mirroring interpretation] He was full of shit!

P14: [Ignoring my interpretation and reverting to his usual intellectual rumination] They [his bosses] have a screwy idea of taking inventory twice a month and using part-time help. What the hell do I care?

T14: [Mirroring interpretation] It's all shit.

P15: [Ignoring me] I got a new job now. [Pauses. Then agrees] It is—there is a lot of shit involved—a lot of waste of time. [Pause. Wearily] A lot of waste of time and energy. [He breaks contact with me and reverts to his usual self-absorbed obsessional free associating for 2-1/2 minutes* before I find an opportunity to interrupt, even though his question is purely rhetorical]. . . . What am I getting involved in all that crap for?

T15: It's all shit.

P16: [But he ignores my interruption and continues for another 2 minutes until I again interrupt, when he says] So I *have* the feeling that it's all shit. I feel like givin' up and cryin' or something—or doing some fuckin' thing. . . .

T16: [Mirroring interpretation] Shit or get off the pot! [Getting off the pot is giving up]

P17: [Hesitates. Sighs.] What do you mean shit or get off the pot? Give or get off the pot?

T17: *Shit* or get off the pot!

P18: What does shit mean in this respect?

T18: Shit! Shit! Shit!

P19: [Laughs] Fuck you! [Having failed to entice me into intellectualizing he resumes free associating in an almost inaudible tone for one minute and a half, ending by saying] . . . Which proves my point.

T19: [Mirroring interpretation] Which proves you're full of shit.

P20: [Finally piqued] It proves *you're* full of shit!

T20: [Mirroring] *You're* full of shit.

P21: *You're* full of shit, because I ought to know how I act when the anxiety sets in.

T21: You're still full of shit.

P22: [Exasperated. Again tries to intellectualize] My anxiety sets in with sex. Even when I was a kid. And it's a constant thing!

---

*For the sake of brevity selected portions of the protocol containing repetitive and rambling ruminations have been omitted. These, while perhaps interesting from a case history point of view, do not add to any understanding of the treatment strategy being demonstrated.

T22: [Not responding to intellectual content] Your anxiety is shit!

P23: [Laughs] I don't give a fuck what you call it. My anxiety is there, it's a feeling . . .

T23: It's shit!

P24: [Overriding me] . . . inside me.

T24: [Louder] You're full of shit!

P25: I'm afraid of something or other.

T25: You're afraid of shitting.

P26: I'm afraid of shitting . . .

T26: . . . shitting in your pants. [This refers to a traumatic incident in his childhood]

P27: [Seizes upon this interpretation eagerly] That's fear. Shitting in your pants is caused by fear.

T27: Fear is caused by shitting in your pants.

P28: Well, one kind of fear engenders another kind.

T28: It's *all* shit.

P29: You're sort of starting to get me angry. What do you mean it's all shit?

T29: [Loudly] All shit!

P30: It's all shit. [Transference is now acknowledged preconsciously] You remind me of the old man. It was all shit with him. He was full of shit. Mad at everybody—angry in the house—scaring the shit out of me to the point where I couldn't even make up my own mind, make up my own opinions. I had the feeling I had to get along with him. All that shit made me anxious. I wanted to destroy him and no doubt I left the house and never went back because of that. . . . [starts rambling but I interrupt after one minute] . . . and that stupid fuckin' Helen had a certain soft whining character like my mother, threw me for a fuckin' loop . . .

T30: [Mirroring interpretation] Soft shit! [Soft whining]

P31: Diarrhea. Soft shit. [Mumbles to himself]

T31: Shit!

P32: Shit makes me think.

T32: That's right. You've got a head full of shit. [Mirroring his very low self-regard]

P33: [Laughs] So you're not able to define it otherwise except shit.

T33: Shit is shit. [This is infantile logic]

P34: Who's to determine whether shit is less valuable than anything else? [Obviously trying to get a debate going]

T34: Shit is the most valuable thing in the world. Nothing more valuable than shit. [This mirrors the infantile unconscious]

P35: I don't know about that. [Trying to be reasonable] Shit is excretion, waste—has no further use for the person. Makes me think of shit, something I've been forced to make. I don't know. I don't

give a fuck. I've reached a point where my personal rationaliza-
tions no longer serve me and I'm sort of ready to admit I don't
know what the fuck is going on. . . . [His resistance is starting to
dissolve. Slips into mumbling to himself and ruminating for about
4 minutes, offering a variety of tempting interpretations for me to
bite on. Finally] So there! *You're* full of shit. It *is* caused by sex.

T35: [Mirroring] You're full of shit!

P36: [Angrily] *You're* full of shit!

T36: [Mirroring. Louder] *You're* full of shit!

P37: You're full of shit because I should know what feelings come upon
me in certain situations.

T37: You don't know from shit.

P38: I know that much. I know that some feeling comes up, a confused
feeling, an anxious feeling, fear, some fuckin' thing. If you want
to use the word, anxiety. All this is anxiety.

T38: You know shit.

P39: [Like a smart child] But you said shit's very valuable stuff.

T39: That's a lot of shit. You know a lot of shit.

P40: You're full of horseshit because I should be able to function with
these women where I'd feel free and full of affection.

T40: [Alluding to a communication from a previous session] You'd shit
all over them.

P41: So that's the point! I want to shit all over them. That's where the
anxiety comes in. See!? So you're full of shit. So that's what I've
been saying here. [Warming up] I'd like to shit all over them! Call
them fucking names! Tell them they're no fuckin' good, like the
old man did. [With relish] Maybe slap them around and pull their
fuckin' hair and kick them! That's most likely what I'd want to do
to them.

T41: [Mirroring] Shit on them!

P42: [Loudly punching out each word] *And shit on them—and piss on
them. And do everything* I heard the old man say, that I hated so
much.

T42: [Mirroring] He shit on everybody.

P43: He shit on my mother and me, I'll tell you that much—sure shit
on us. Reminds me of some guy that I laid into. Every time he sees
me now he has to play up to me. That's the way I was with the old
man.

T43: [Mirroring] Scared shit!

P44: Scared shit is right. That big bastard would come down and beat
the shit out of you. That's right. [With emphasis] That t'is right!
Scared shit and paralyzed. My mind would dynamically operate to
where I could placate this bastard. Fuckin' bastard! That's why I
hate bullies. I plot. I plot how to bring the bastards down. I guess

that's the reason politics appeals to me. [Pause] That's right. I'm still the little boy—operating toward women with all the fuckin' fear of God and sin,—and actually wanting to be like the old man—cursing 'em—because if I curse them and dispense with them there wouldn't be any sin involved. Let them go to hell or something. [Pounding the couch with his fist in frustration and rage] Who the hell knows what the whole fuckin' thing is anyway? Fuck you! I feel like breaking your couch, [chuckles with pleasure] coming down on the fuckin' thing and destroying it, and destroying *you with it*!—A fuckin' cyclone—Hit this fuckin'place and send all those books and fans and everything in this place whirling up into a spiral! Wreck the fuckin' joint like I wrecked Germany in—[Sighs]—And then I bring myself back to reality, the world being what it is. [Calmly] In a sense, try to remain objective in the face of all the laws that operate in the situation. Certain situations are bigger than I am. [His voice trails off into a self-absorbed almost inaudible mumble for awhile. Then his voice becomes audible]. . . . I think of myself as shit. Coming back to your term, shit. I have a very poor estimate of myself. I don't behave with principle and honesty. I don't seem to function well with men *or* women—or in any situation without being moved by these fuckin' hostile feelings. [Groans loudly] In a sense you could say I hate myself.

T44: [Mirroring interpretation] You treat yourself like shit!

P45: So you fuckin' bum, you're so smart. Why do I treat myself like shit for?

T45: Because you feel like a piece of shit.

P46: [Very reasonably] So that doesn't answer the question. It's still the same question. Why do I treat myself or *feel* like a piece of shit?

T46: Because you're full of shit!

P47: [Disgusted and frustrated with me] Oh, you're full of shit. [Decides to analyze] I know some of the reasons why. Because I feel like I treated my mother and father with no respect, especially my mother. I shouldn't have run away from home when I did. I should have . . .

T47: [A communication from a previous session] She had shit in her crotch!

P48: So she had shit in her crotch.

T48: [Again repeating a communication from a previous session] She was always scratching her shitty crotch.

P49: So what? [He is now defending what he previously attacked] Anybody does that.

T49: [I now mirror his previous attack on his father from another session] Your old man threw shit out of the window.

P50: [With guilt and anguish] I wasn't back for their funerals. Oh what a fuckin' son I was. Just ran away from them. [Sadly and emotionally] I wanted to get away from them and I finally did. I didn't want to go back to the same obstinate scenes. The same obstinate scene that made me function in the last election. Well fuck it! I couldn't help it. I was harassed. [He begins mumbling about a survey he made during the recent election but I interrupt]

T50: [Mirroring interpretation] It was full of bullshit.

P51: What was full of bullshit?

T51: Your report was full of bullshit!

P52: [Very logically and matter of fact] It wasn't filled with bullshit. It was filled with condensed matter.

T52: [Persisting] That's what shit is, condensed matter.

P53: [Continuing his intellectualizing] Almost anything can be described as condensed matter. Shit comes from all different kinds of things. . . . [Voice trails off into a mumble and he drifts into almost inaudible self-pitying ruminations for about 6 minutes]. . . . So what the hell can I do? Nothin'! [60 seconds of silence] Why the hell should I tell you anything when all you do is keep saying it's all shit. It's all shit. [Challengingly] So, if it's all shit, then whatever I say must be shit too.

T53: [Mirroring his obstinacy] That's right.

P54: So why the fuck should I talk? [Laughs]

T54: Shit or get off the pot.

P55: [Mimicking] Shit or get off the pot. Shit or get off the pot. I don't even know what the hell it means. [Sighs]

T55: I know what it means, don't worry.

P56: Shit or get off the pot. What does it mean in this specific situation?

T56: [Mirroring his lack of cooperation] I'm not telling you.

P57: You're not telling me? Why aren't you telling me?

T57: [Mirroring his obstinacy] Why should I tell you?

P58: Because I want to know.

T58: That's no reason for me to tell you.

P59: [Incredulously] What?

T59: That's a reason for you, not for me.

P60: [Laughs] What is this? We're supposed to be working together here. [We have now reversed positions: a typical outcome when the resistance-joining tactic is successful]

T60: Who?

P61: You and I. [Laughs] I thought we were working with each other.

T61: [Joining with his resistance] I thought we were working against each other.

P62: [In disbelief] What?!

T62: I thought we were working against each other.

P63: [Amused] Or working together—What the hell's the difference.

T63: No difference?

P64: I'm here. [Pause] What's your interpretation of working against each other?

T64: *My* interpretation? [Like a nagging parent] I've told you a thousand times!

P65: [After a moment's thought] Well, just because I'm working against you, it's no reason for you to be working against me.

T65: Why not?

P66: [Glibly] Because I don't know any better. That's the way I've been raised and conditioned . . .

T66: [Joining his resistance] I don't expect you to know any better.

P67: . . . to work against things. To be agin' em—like the old man was agin' em. That's the only reaction I can get in contact with.

T67: [Double-binding him] The only way to cure you is to work against you. [Addressing his negative suggestibility] I'll never get your cooperation.

P68: So when there are little streaks of cooperation why in the hell do you knock it down for?

T68: [Mirroring his defiance] Who needs it? I don't need your cooperation.

P69: [His resistance is dissolving] I need it.

T69: What do you need it for?

P70: [Like a child] I need things explained to me.

T70: [Relenting] What do you want explained?

P71: I clean forgot what I originally asked you.

T71: [Mirroring] You got shit for brains.

P72: [Laughs] Ah . . .

T72: [Mirroring interpretation] You don't know what you want.

P73: I don't even want to ask you anymore. Fuck you! You remind me of all the characters I met throughout my life, mostly negative. I didn't understand the hostile bastards. The really friendly ones—I can almost remember every one and I reacted very favorably to them. But the hostile ones, I acted just like I acted to the old man—and I couldn't openly oppose them because they were all bigger than I was and I was afraid of them and I would just harbor resentment. It makes me feel hopeless and helpless. [Almost in tears] I feel like crying. So what's the use of trying to make up to the old man? I have that feeling very strong now. [This is a transference communication] There's nothing but disappointment. [Pause] Some of these politicians [i.e., psychoanalysts]—I react to them in the same way that I did to the old man. [Sighs] So I'm saying to myself, "What the hell. I must still be holding out in the sense of wishing the old man would react differently." [This is a transference communication. He wants me to react differently]

T73: How do [sic] you want him to react? [i.e., How do you want me to react?]

P74: [The resistance has now been resolved] With affection and understanding.

T74: [Using the patient as a consultant] How would he do that?

P75: What?

T75: How would he do that? What would he do?

P76: Oh, pay more attention to me, when I was younger. [He wants me to pay more attention to him.]

T76: [Seeking instructions] What would he do now?

P77: Now? I don't know what he possibly could do now, outside of being friendly and affectionate.

T77: [Asking for specific instructions] How would he show his friendliness and affection?

P78: [Like a child] By talking to me.

T78: What would he talk to you about?

P79: About being friendly.

T79: How would he show his friendliness?

P80: Most likely he'd ask me about something I was doing. How I was making out. If he would say something like that, I'd feel like crying.

T80: [Following his instructions] Well, how are you making out?

P81: [Earnestly] Well, in my work I'm making out essentially all right.

T81: [With paternal concern] Everything all right at work?

P82: Yeah, everything is essentially okay at my job. Yes.

T82: [Showing interest] Are you pleased with your new assignment?

P83: Yeah, and I know my boss has a lot of confidence in me. Knows I'm loyal and faithful and would fight like a tiger for him.

T83: [Showing regard] I have a lot of confidence in you.

P84: [Moved] Shit!

T84: You're a very loyal guy.

P85: [Silent for 15 seconds] This harassing of me during the last election, by my boss, completely threw me off.

T85: [Reflecting] He hurt you. You're very sensitive. You can't work without love.

P86: I can work without love but give me a little reason for crissake. [His voice trails off about his father's negativity and the current parallels in his work situation for two and a half minutes] . . . and anyway there's my analysis. Maybe I can get some idea of why I function as I do. It's rough going.

T86:   [Sympathetically] What's rough?

P87:   Aw, it's rough. I don't get anything positive out of life. [Pause] I
       don't feel close to anybody. [I don't feel close to you] I'm wary, I
       guess. I'm suspicious.

T87:   [Mirroring] Well, I'd like to get close to you.

P88:   Well, I'd like to get close to you, but I don't know how the fuck to
       do it. [Pause] My first reaction is to push you away like I have ev-
       erybody else. So what the hell can I do? [Sighs. 45 second silence.
       Therapist rises]

T88:   Thank you. [Session is over]

*   *   *

No resistance, once resolved, departs forever never to return. Transference resistances, especially negative narcissistic transference resistances,
are particularly problematic to work with. To be able to observe such a
resistance resolve even temporarily is reward enough. In my experience,
progress in treatment is measured in small increments, not giant breakthroughs, and each session presents technical problems that must be managed in their own right (Lennard & Bernstein, 1960).

Unfortunately, after this milestone session in the treatment Jack and I
had only one more opportunity to meet before we took our summer break
and so it was not possible to exploit fully the gains we seem to have made
in this session. Nevertheless Jack continued in treatment for 5 more
years. He had been in his 50s when he began treatment and he was in his
60s when he ended. He had always been very angry and anxiety ridden
and the fear of homosexuality was never far from his mind. And so it
went over the years. He came regularly, growled and swore his way
through his sessions, complained about me and his dissatisfaction with
the treatment—and his symptoms gradually subsided. In particular, there
was a marked decrease in his anxiety level, and the fear that he would
throw himself out of a window (his main presenting problem) disap-
peared completely.

Needless to say, strategies such as those implemented in this case must
be used sparingly and with great circumspection, and even then, only after a therapeutic alliance has been firmly established. They should never
be used when the therapist is emotionally involved nor as a disguised
means for acting out hostility or impatience. Therefore, before they can
be safely used, they must be carefully monitored and analyzed for any
contamination from subjective countertransference sources.

Alas, a fuller elaboration of the psychodynamics underlying the phenomenon of mirroring must await another occasion. Theoretical progress
best rests upon the bedrock foundation of clinical discovery.

REFERENCES

Bernstein, A. (1965). The psychoanalytic technique. In B.B. Wolman (Ed.), *Handbook of clinical psychology* (pp. 1168-1199). New York: McGraw Hill.

Coleman, M. L. (1956). Externalization of the toxic introject: A treatment technique for borderline cases. *The Psychoanalytic Review, 43*(2), 235-242.

Lennard, H. L., & Bernstein, A. (1960). *Anatomy of psychotherapy.* New York: Columbia University.

Sherman, M. (1968). Play-fantasy and gratification in psychotherapy. In M. C. Nelson et al., *Roles and paradigms in psychotherapy* (pp. 192-217). New York: Grune & Stratton.

Spotnitz, H. (1963). The toxoid response. *The Psychoanalytic Review, 50*(4), 611-624.

Spotnitz, H. (1969). *Modern psychoanalysis of the schizophrenic patient.* New York: Grune & Stratton.

Spotnitz, H., & Meadow, P. W. (1976). *Treatment of the narcissistic neuroses.* New York: Manhattan Center for Advanced Psychoanalytic Studies.

Comment

It's not often that one has an opportunity to read the kind of verbatim report of a psychotherapy session that Dr. Bernstein offers us in his article. I was amused when I thought of what my reaction would have been when I was a fledgling therapist—or even several years ago. I would have been shocked and offended by the language to begin with, to say nothing of the author's behavior toward his patient. It certainly wasn't the way I was "brought up" to do psychotherapy. What would Carl Rogers say? Where was that total acceptance, unconditional positive regard, nonpossessive warmth, and accurately empathic understanding he considered essential for effective therapy? Certainly not here. I would have said something like, "Where does he get off, treating a person like that? How dare he? If anyone treated me that way my reaction would be, 'Who needs this? For *this* I'm paying my hard-earned money?'" And I'd get up and walk out. That would have been the end of *that* therapist. But that was before I knew about modern psychoanalysis.

Almost as if anticipating such reactions, Dr. Bernstein tells us that "In spite of the fact that for years I maintained a consistently accepting, noncritical, nonjudgmental attitude toward him and listened patiently [and] After years of 'analytic neutrality' and of being a 'blank screen,' I had not succeeded. . . ." Those were stances I'd also been taught. But they didn't work. "If at first you don't succeed," exhorts the old adage, "try, try again." But how long do you keep trying the same old thing? I like someone's addition to that adage, "If again you don't succeed, give up." Try something different. Dr. Bernstein tried something different.

No one can know with any certainty how appropriate or effective a particular intervention will be. Sometimes interventions sincerely meant in the best interests of the patient are experienced as narcissistic injuries. So I admire Dr. Bernstein's courage in attempting and revealing his "heroic measure." Perhaps now, especially to those familiar with paradoxical and paradigmatic approaches and with modern psychoanalysis, there is nothing new here, nothing particularly heroic. But at the time this interview took place, before encounter groups and confrontive techniques were as common as they are now, this was a truly innovative strategy.

He tried something different, specifically tailored for this patient. Different strokes for different folks. Like the doctor of homeopathy who administers minute doses of a remedy that would in healthy persons produce symptoms of the disease in order to build up immunity and eventually lead to cure, the author gave his patient "carefully titrated doses of his own medicine to stimulate a sort of psychic toxoid response and immunize his ego. . . ." The language—well, that was Jack's language, one he understood well and one that could could convey layers of meaning to him. He also knew the behavior well since it was his own. But the test of the pudding is in the eating. The results tell us the effectiveness of a particular intervention. I was fascinated as I watched the process unfold. The author stayed on his course—in spite of all of Jack's efforts to steer him away—and did not allow himself to get "hooked" by what might appear at first glance to be important insights or exploration; and he avoided Jack's forays into self-analysis that served as resistance. Mirroring and joining techniques evoked a variety of reactions: surprise, curiosity, bewilderment, anger, defiance. Energy built up as interventions led to productive progressive communications on Jack's part.

I was moved when Jack finally spoke—in such a different tone—about his disappointment in his father, and the way in which Dr. Bernstein picked this up and asked for instructions about how to proceed. When Jack went back into his past—that analytic going back, back to a backness that cannot be changed—he avoided that futile quest and kept Jack in the present, "What would he say, do?" here, now. And then he "became" the father, here, now, which led to Jack's final admission of his loneliness and longing for closeness and his despair of ever achieving it. We see in this interview a glimpse of the journey Mark Stern refers to in his article earlier in this issue in which he speaks of Izette de Forest's description of the course of the analytic venture: "anger and then love."

My fantasy/wish was that this first major breakthrough after years of therapy would have been a beginning of a continuing process of unfolding, growth, and change leading to final resolution of conflict. So it was sobering to have the author point out just what it was: This milestone session was simply a major breakthrough *at that moment*. Reality in the form of a long interruption of therapy intervened. We'll never know what would have happened if it had not. Breakthroughs are not magic cures effecting instant transformation. They are simply the opening, hopefully the first step toward deeper work, and we are reminded that lasting progress is still "measured in small increments over a period of time."

I couldn't help but be curious about Dr. Bernstein's own reactions during his work with Jack. After all, he'd taken this kind of abuse for years. Even when one is aware that Jack's abrasiveness and aggressiveness toward him were transferential in nature, they were still abrasive. Some therapists might have felt, "Who needs this kind of abuse? Enough is enough!" I appreciate that the author is a skilled seasoned therapist, but even skilled seasoned therapists have reality-based reactions, to say nothing of countertransferential ones as well.

"Needless to say," we are cautioned at the end of this article, "strategies such as those implemented in this case must be used sparingly and with great circumspection." Well, maybe it's not so needless to say after all. Not everybody would be comfortable using this approach—me, for example. For others it could be only too natural and easy a way of dealing with abrasive patients.

I respect any clinician who is willing to reveal in detail just what it is that he or she does in the privacy of the office. I appreciate the learning experience that this article has been for me and I hope that it will be so for others too.

Genevieve Izinicki

Tradition and Dogma
in the Experience of Abrasion

Marie Coleman Nelson

Had I been invited to write about abrasive patients 30 years ago I would have developed an essay in which all the data were examined from the classical standpoint of transference and countertransference. Even today the notion of transference and countertransference excludes a number of elements which profoundly affect both patient and clinician in their work but receive slight attention because they are "givens" in the situation.

I will not deal here with such abrasive stimuli as mannerisms and peculiarities, or modes of defense that are particularly (sometimes literally) odious to the therapist but nevertheless familiar to us all. Instead, I will try to point to the manner in which certain temporal, social, and cultural factors with their implicit mandates operate as instigators of abrasion and also as agencies for the suppression of open communication on topics that challenge the Establishment.

THE CONSPIRACY OF SILENCE ABOUT ABRASIVE PATIENTS

While an occasional client will strain the tolerance of a succession of therapists equally, clinicians vary greatly in their definition of, and response to, abrasiveness. I have related comfortably to patients who had proven intolerable to previous therapists. Other clinicians report the same hence one cannot rule out the auspicious, even mysterious, element of "fit" in therapeutic arrangements.

On the whole, clinicians refrain from publishing extensively on the experience of being abraded, though they may complain or even make rueful jokes about it to trusted colleagues. Readers of technical essays are generally obliged to draw their own conclusions from case studies that shroud the gory details on abrasive patients in dispassionate analyses of transference resistance and the methods employed to resolve the patient's

Marie Coleman Nelson, co-founder with her late husband, Professor Benjamin Nelson, of Paradigmatic Psychotherapy, is Honorary Editor of *The Psychotherapy Patient* and past Editor of *The Psychoanalytic Review*. Ms. Nelson now practices and teaches in Kenya.

problems. Frank admissions of abrasive inductions by patients are more likely to be found among therapists who acknowledge ego-strengthening aspects in the expression of aggression (Eigen, 1983; Little, 1951; Racker, 1957; Searles, 1965; Spotnitz & Meadow, 1976) and clinicians who employ encounter techniques.

Certainly, tolerance of abrasion and even its acknowledgment in human relations depend as much on cultural variables as on personal sensitivity and the length of one's fuse, so to speak. A case in point: Only recently in our Nairobi newspaper there appeared an account of a 50-year-old grandmother sentenced to prison for killing her 4-year-old grandson by striking him on the head with a rock. She had reportedly tolerated three beatings by her son and a fourth by his wife, but what angered her most and prompted her to commit the crime was "when the child's mother told me to go and sleep with her husband who is my own son" (*Daily Nation*, 8/2/83).

In the course of evolution the *word* has become as potent as the *act*, and since the spoken word is the prime identifiable avenue of communication between the therapist and client, it may prove useful to examine various civilizational influences that work behind the scenes in our own culture to maintain a conspiracy of silence on the question of abrasiveness in treatment.

1. Health and Wealth

Anticipating the contemporary emphasis in Lacanian (French) psychoanalysis on semiotics, Feuer (1955) stressed the importance of linguistic usage as the principal overt indicator of what is considered good or bad in different cultures. He proposed as a general principle that "corresponding to different social structures with their different personality-forms, there will likewise be diverse ethical languages, each with its specific characterization" (p. 21). Citing a number of examples testifying to the vulnerability of Americans to advertising and promotional campaigns, Feuer asks, "Need we then be surprised when the philosophical analyst in American culture tells us that the meaning of 'good' is its emotive persuasiveness?" (p. 21).

Emotive persuasiveness, which plays a large part in our predilection for millennial cults, fads and fancies, instant therapies, and peculiar preferences with respect to political candidates, is without doubt a sanctioned quality in American life. But it is Feuer's emphasis on ethical languages and their implicit sanctions that interests us here, for operating within these structures ourselves we do not question them. And parallel to emotive suggestibility, of which we are all more or less aware, runs the sterner imperative of rationalism. In a comparative essay on the concept of self, Johnson (1982) finds that Western psychology and philosophy have shown a distinct preference for analytic . . . and static descriptions of self as a series of complex relationships involving internalized, standardized, elements which are universally observable in human beings. Within such standardization, "normal" behavior has been judged to be that which pursues plausible and legitimized objectives, although subject to some modification based on age, custom, and situation. Similarly, "normal" thought is considered to have qualities of coherence, syllogistic relevance and internal consistency. Thought and behavior that deviated from these hypothetical and idealized standards are regarded as irrational, that is to say, pathological.

The implicit definition of "good" is shaped by collective interests — "givens" — over which the individual exerts no control, due to psychosocial repression (Freedman, 1939) and/or because his* tangible needs are shaped and served by allegiance to the collective definitions of good and bad held by his professional, political, economic, social, and religious reference group. Commenting on the close alliance of psychoanalysis with social action, both as doctrine and therapy, during the 60s in France, Turkle (1978) offers a retrospective comparison of this movement with the historical direction taken by American psychoanalysis:

> Torn from its base in the cultural sciences by an early (1927) decision by the American Psychoanalytic Association to limit the practice of psychoanalysis to medical doctors, American psychoanalysis became a psychiatric, medical and even corporate "insider." In its theoretical development it favored a psychoanalytic ego psychology where the predominant model is of a therapeutic alliance between the egos of analyst and patient in the service of a better adaptation to reality. American psychoanalysis was socialized, or perhaps, domesticated by American institutions and values. Although some analysts did use psychoanalytic insights as part of a critique of American life, they were exceptions to the general trend.

This despite the fact that "in Freud's work are formulations of psychoanalysis as radical doctrine with an implicit critique of social repression," Turkle comments.

There is no question in the mind of this writer that regardless of whether the American therapist wishes to reflect this accommodative model (assuming that he takes note of it) his status in the eye of the profession demands it. He is considered ineffectual if his fees are not esca-

---

*In generalizing here and elsewhere I intend the masculine pronominal to apply also to the female sex. When grammarians contrive a general third-person form as alternative to the clumsy "he/she" I will be among the first to use it.

lated along with those of his peers and incapable of maintaining a private practice if he continues working in a clinic setting at a relatively lower income, out of genuine interest in low-income patients. When I first began to supervise candidates I was chided by a senior colleague in my association for rendering supervision at a slightly lower fee than others who were more experienced. The middle-class patient lives according to similar dictates; I was once sharply reproached by a female patient for failing to dress "opulently" (thus to enhance her image of a therapist worth her salt), and reprimanded years later by two ex-patients, both of whom became psychiatrists, for having adjusted my fees commensurate with their limited funds when they were university students. By so doing, both claimed independently that I had not made their therapies so critically important that they were obliged to "suffer enough." I was less abraded by the charge than by the fact that their moving in the "higher" circles of the medical echelon had transformed them into caste-conscious fatheads. Indeed, I would have relished the opportunity to make up their lost suffering. Such instances have helped me to understand why so many case presentations sound like financial news: "The patient has bought a house . . . found a more lucrative job . . . demanded a raise . . . persuaded his wife to go to work . . . found a rich boy friend," and so forth. They also reveal unquestioning acceptance by clinicians of the cultural injunction to identify with its definition of success that underlies the technical stance of neutrality toward the patient's "success-oriented" treatment objectives. While we may strive, for the sake of the family's life together, to modify a client's workaholic climb up the ladder of success, we do not question the cultural imperatives that establish his work pattern. Thus, the few patients who eschew the Gospel of Horatio Alger without providing their therapists some secondary gain of reflected glory through other types of creative achievement are very likely to abrade these clinicians by inducing in them the feeling that they have failed to normalize the patient according to the prevailing standard of reality.

2. The Medical Model

Related to the implicit equation of upward mobility with mental health is the implicit assumption that the successful therapist has achieved mental health and is therefore in no need of intrapsychic change (Nelson, 1962). This stance, particularly evident in clinicians who unquestioningly subscribe to the manipulative medical model that casts them in the role of potters, the patients as clay, and the treatment as the wheel,* opposes and

---

*In the Third World unfavorable conditions such as minimal staffing, overwork, and insufficient training in psychodynamic principles conspire to reinforce the authoritarian self-image and reliance on medication for symptomatic relief.

subtly stigmatizes the minority of colleagues who openly (though of course selectively) acknowledge patient-induced thoughts, feelings, and fantasies in their sessions at various points in treatment. Clinicians with inordinate investment in professional status view such disclosures as evidence of self-indulgence, weakness rather than strength, even though these communications provide valuable insight into the deeper emotional needs of both participants as well as cues for progressive interventions.

In a fascinating published dialogue (Langs & Searles, 1980) Langs says to Searles:

> You are, in my experience, one of the few analysts who provides me with ideas that go beyond the hard core of current psychoanalytic thought, and who stimulates in me definitely creative responses, as well. . . .
>
> This relates to our unfinished discussion, a moment ago, regarding the mainstream of American psychoanalysis and those who are not in the mainstream. It is my impression that it is in the analysts who are far more creative, and far more into—in terms of technique and the clinical situation—into interaction, who are on the periphery, while those analysts who can restate the old theory in ways that deceptively seem original are the heroes, as I would put it, of the main body of analysts, such as the echelon of the American Psychoanalytic Association [Langs, 1978, Ch. 3]. And our literature reflects this deadness or sterility; there are few papers today which touch in a very meaningful way on unique aspects of the analytic and therapeutic interactions that need yet to be understood and resolved. (p. 78)

Thus, not only the medical model but also conformity to imposed culture cues, professional guidelines, and theoretical dicta concerning the nature of treatment and the manner in which it is ideally conducted conspire to the impoverishment of literature on the clinician's reactions of abrasiveness. Given the limit on self-expression within which he must work, these must be frequent and intense.

3. Paradoxical Attitudes Toward Aging

Unlike less advanced cultures in which age-group traditions still inform interpersonal relations, Americans largely subscribe to the inductions of their society to live and think "young" beyond their chronological years, and for valid and understandable reasons postpone for as long as possible the day when they must face the senium, segregated from heterogeneous society. The relatively affluent psychotherapeutic community endorses the youth cult. Male analysts divorce their aging wives for younger women, while their female counterparts are as concerned as their lay sisters with face-lifts, health spas, vitamins, hormones, and diets.

Nevertheless, it has always seemed to this writer that psychoanalysts and psychotherapists must encounter aging problems of somewhat different quality and magnitude then do most professionals and laymen, since continuous work with psychic process and affective material fosters deep attunement to the symbolic and overt attitudes of colleagues as well as patients toward themselves. With the onset of old age this very capacity may serve self-abrasive ends on two counts:

First, with respect to the clinician's role vis-à-vis colleagues: Assuming that he has fully participated in teaching, supervision, writing, holding office, and so forth, the older therapist has typically developed some area of specialization or theoretical interest and identified fairly consistently with known positions in organizational politics. Not particularly realizing it, he comes to be viewed as a "gray eminence" and is repeatedly called upon to reiterate themes already familiar to his contemporaries if not to younger associates. He is no longer perceived in his own right, but is increasingly seen as an embodiment of the group's history, a repository of its arcana.

Among students he is received with a mixture of awe and even subservience. He is accorded more influence than he truly possesses and probably more knowledge as well. If he lectures or presents a paper many questions tempt him to exhume his earlier views rather than relating to some fresh theme he may introduce. Indeed, moving beyond these prior concepts may even disappoint his listeners, since his earlier works acquire oracular reification and twice-told tales have their own soporific charm. A collusion develops: The gray eminence, deferring to the inductions of the group, dons the mantle of distinction. This honor is not devoid of ambivalent components in that it tends to isolate him from everyday participation in the politics of the association, reserving him for delicate mediatorial functions and as a drawing card at professional events. Narcissistically inflated through the feedback process, he becomes congealed in a static posture and is gradually transformed into a caricature of himself. Aging therapists who find this merged group/self-image inauthentic and restrictive—even abrasive—are prone to withdraw from participation and only a very few continue to function benignly, impervious to transformative pressures. The latter (or so it seems to me) are individuals who have always operated within a broader and more flexible frame of theoretical and clinical reference which accommodates to changing emphases and new approaches.

Secondly, with respect to the latent problem of generational disparity in the treatment of younger adults: This is obviously an area that analysts, in particular, are not only reluctant to discuss but rationalize in a number of ways. Confrontation with the problem involves the recall of abrasive encounters in the therapeutic situation, which certainly points to the necessity for expanding our conceptual horizons in the direction of social and civilizational issues.

During my last 10 years of full-time practice in the United States, six women entered treatment with the ostensible goal of improving their marriages or opting for divorce if this proved impossible. Four were from upper-middle-class backgrounds, all had university educations, none came from broken homes, and none had any history of homosexual experiences. Four were employed professionals and two were working toward graduate degrees. All but one couple had one or more children ranging in age from one to ten years. The husbands were professionals and industrial engineers. Although the women were dissimilar they shared in common extremes of acting-out behavior against the marital relationship, militantly justified on grounds that they were "Liberated."

These patients generated strong feelings of dismay, revulsion, and anger in me. I felt as though we—they and I—had been reared on separate planets, since the only value they seemed to cherish was the actualization of fantasy. It would be tedious to elaborate on their treatment, but it is necessary to mention in summary fashion the quality of their behavior inside the therapy in order to communicate what, exactly, I found so repellent.

The youngest and least affluent of the group, who could not afford baby sitters for her child, quite seriously solicited my support in a full-time campaign she had carried on for several months before coming into treatment to win her husband's agreement that her lover live with them in the home; not only—as she told the husband—because she had "enough [i.e., sex] to go around," but because "someone would always be home to take care of the baby." My preassigned role, I learned, was to persuade the husband of the reasonableness of her plan, "otherwise I will have to divorce him and put the baby with my mother."

The second patient, who characterized herself as grossly misunderstood by her husband in her earnest search for identity, drove him out of the house with hysterical temper tantrums and tailed him secretly in her car with the expectation of catching him in an act of infidelity as he made his business rounds.

The third patient, wife of a doctor, picked up men and had sex with them in motels. She had also embarked on a campaign of silence and communicated with the husband through the maid or in written notes. She was satisfied with the arrangement but the husband was not, and she really wanted help in getting him to leave the house so that she could feel free.

Wife Four resented her husband's social popularity, hated his profession, locked him out of the apartment, cut up all his clothes, dumped them into the public hall, and falsely reported him to the I.R.S. as an income-tax evader. (This husband had committed the ultimate provocation by laughing at her insistent demands that he accept a more lucrative directorship in a field which held no interest for him.)

Wife Five, whose education had been subsidized by her husband and who was seen once weekly with him and once alone, opened her private session one day with the triumphant announcement, "Well, I've got my degree and I've got a job. He's served his purpose and you've served yours. I'm leaving. He can keep coming, he'll be all right. You can have him . . . I don't want him!" (My instant reply, "You can't dump him on me. He's your responsibility, not mine. If you leave I won't see him again, either," apparently had some effect, for whatever reason. Though she flounced out and neither returned, I heard indirectly several years later that they stayed together and now have a child.)

The sixth woman complained so convincingly of her husband's inability to relate that I pictured him as being severely depressed or becoming schizophrenic. When at my suggestion she brought him to treatment he turned out to be intellectual, witty, with a sardonic sense of humor and an unconcealed attitude of scorn toward psychoanalysis as an unscientific discipline, yet seriously willing to participate in therapy to improve the marriage. His wife's gloomy portrait was in part a reflection of her own difficulties but accurate in the sense that all contact between them had turned so abrasive that it led to further alienation. As the husband opened up with her (her claimed need) she became more secretive with him, and when he carried out his share of agreed household chores she defaulted increasingly on hers. When she finally declared (in a private session) her intention to begin a sexual affair with a male colleague I refused to continue treating both herself and her husband (I did not collude secretly with one marital partner against another in such situations), but indicated that having been the initial patient she had first priority to remain. She chose to be the one to leave. Subsequently I learned through the husband's ongoing treatment that when his wife told him of her affair and tried to bring her lover into the home openly, indicating that she expected him to accept the arrangement and "make friends" with the man, he moved out and a divorce followed. He later remarried, having benefited greatly from treatment (and he also revised his opinion about psychoanalysis).

Abrasive patients are like castor oil. They are awful to take, but if you can stomach them they purge a great deal of self-delusion. I will mention at the outset that I ordinarily welcome patients' expression of all feelings, and although I have reservations about "official" psychoanalysis today, I continue to believe that the analysis of feelings and their ideational correlates by whatever talking techniques prove viable, is the essence of therapy. Some 35 years of practice in this mode have made me no stranger to rage and criticism.

Above all, my confidence in my ability to diminish these patients' acting-out, which kept everything communicated so situational and dramatically overheated that the therapies could not be stabilized, was shaken. While all six women were as knowledgeable as most American cosmopolites about analytic procedure, they rarely strayed from substantive critiques of their marital interaction and their husbands' shortcomings, rooted in the feminist myth of psychological parallelism between the sexes and the implicit expectation of total accommodation to their desires. Their reading of all interaction in the light of this dogma produced in me an almost physical discomfort, as though I were confined in a small space from which there was no escape.*

Associated with these elements, the infidelities and deliberate acts of spite and failed cooperation, justified in the name of self-fulfillment by the wives and notably unleavened by remorse (except for the hysterical patient) aroused punitive impulses in me. My interest in understanding the patients became diverted by a growing sense of horrified sympathy for the husbands who were paralyzed by their wives' relentless course, and for the children about whom the mothers spoke very little, usually in relation to scheduling, whereas the fathers spoke of them affectionately and expressed concern for their welfare in the discordant homes. My "benign neutrality" was abraded to the point that I felt like making (but did not) decidedly non-neutral comments, like "Why do you let the bitch get away with it?" or "If I were you I would have slugged her!" I realized all too well that the husbands had also come to maturity in the propagandistic heyday of Women's Liberation. Their campus experiences with girls had indoctrinated them to a more matter-of-fact, less romantic attitude toward the opposite sex than their fathers; they had learned to conceal traces of nurturant protectiveness, tender diminutives, and macho possessiveness. Thus the educated men of this younger generation as well as the women were obeying social mandates which in a deep sense curtailed a whole range of affectional expression and playful behavior. Like political dogmatists the wives were too grim, the husbands too abashed, and lovemaking a ritual dance around the feminist Maypole of orgastic pleasure.

By now I am sure that many readers will feel alienated by my moralistic overtones in describing the six women. To have evaded this implication would have begged the question; the totality of their behavior offended my moral sense. My own conscience would have dictated that, given such contempt for a marital partner, I would have severed the rela-

---

*I do not hold with interpretations that the patients were trying to "imprison me" or "kill me off." True narcissists that they were, I did not exist for them, any more than their hubands existed, as a person in my own right, but rather as an extension of themselves hired to help them actualize their fantasies. I do equate the "small-space" image on my part to a coffin, associated with their own repressed fear of death which will be discussed later in this essay.

tionship rather than played such sadistic games. I have felt the same rage with patients who beat their pets, but have at least had the small consolation that victimization of the animals spared some member of the family a murderous assault. The superego is always the battleground for conflict between the generations. Similarly, I found it extremely difficult to empathize with the patients' fundamentally static position beneath their busy "enactments"; to use Lifton's (1976) concept, their inability to "center" or "decenter":

> Decentering is necessary to the continual process of altering the existing forms that constitute the self, and to applying these forms to new encounters in ways that make possible new kinds of psychic experience. In decentering there is a partial suspension of close integration in temporal, spatial and emotional planes, with anticipation of new integrations of a more inclusive kind. The absence of decentering renders the self static, devoid of new content, while absence of centering is associated with inability to connect new experience with viable inner forms. If the self cannot achieve a centering-decentering balance it is unable either to consolidate or to evolve, experience becomes less vivid, and the capacity for ethical conviction (as opposed to moralistic reiteration) diminishes. Centering and decentering, then, are part of a common dialectic, each dependent upon the capacity for grounding. (p. 72)

By the time they entered therapy, their inability to consolidate transformative needs of their own had been compensated for by extensive revisualization of their husbands. Several, aided by prior indoctrinations in feminist consciousness-raising groups, perceived their mates as veritable jailers, ogres bent on breaking their spirits, while four of the women had revisualized the relationship all the way back to their first meeting: "I know now that I only *thought* I loved him," and so forth.

What interested me particularly about the cases was precisely the malevolent symbolic attributes the husbands acquired, and their dehumanization, in the wives' fantasies. Either of two classical hypotheses might be advanced to explain these deteriorated images: One, that due to regression on the part of the women, the husbands gradually assumed the role of fathers in their unconscious and had to be warded off as incestuous objects. The second, based on ample evidence of the wives' narcissistic personalities, that defects in the women's earliest infantile experience of maternal nurture prejudiced their later capacity for close object relationships. Freud's first theory roots psychological difficulties in the oedipal period whereas the second theory, increasingly espoused by orthodox Freudians, assigns them to the mother-infant dyad. (For the sake of brevity these are admittedly crude renditions of highly articulated Freudian propositions.) It was Erikson (1950) who to some extent rescued classical theory from the justified charge of formulating a closed psychobiologic system that allowed no access to social and cultural influences. Erikson's concept of ego development, wherein the acquisition of skills and age-related accomplishments led to altered self-representation and social identification implicitly acknowledged progressive modification of psychic structure throughout life under ordinary circumstances. That such movement could be skewed in various ways he did not question, but he vigorously opposed the use of the word "infantile" in connection with regressive behavior on grounds that such dysfunction bears no similarity to healthy function in infancy (Erikson, 1968).

The history of millennial cults and reform movements provides ample evidence of the cognitive distortions that occur in otherwise rational individuals. Through the mechanisms of projection and displacement, with the emotional support of fellow adherents, those who stand outside the magic circle become the identified enemy. Certainly this was the prevailing atmosphere in feminist "consciousness raising" groups described by a number of other wives in treatment who had briefly participated in them but withdrawn because of their marriage-destructive orientation. But quite apart from such inductions which encouraged the six abrasive wives to nurture demonized images of their husbands, deeper trends in contemporary society foster negative revisualizations in the entire fabric of family life. Surrounded by things of the market place and molded to acquisitive patterns, interpersonal relations also become defined, in the absence of daily life-preservative tasks (such as those with which Third-World poverty populations must cope), in terms of chronic *interpersonal* expectation. Interaction between family members becomes increasingly psychologized. Gestures, attitudes, and remarks that would be shrugged aside as capricious in a more essentialist setting become fair game for interpretation, rumination, and dissection through fantasy elaboration by Western psychological man and woman. Through such amplification relationships acquire a dramaturgic dimension, for in succumbing to the inductions of others the modern family member experiences a split between what he subjectively (and in varying degree mistakenly) believes himself to be—between his "authentic self" and the role self, or selves, into which he feels propelled to meet family demands. In this over-psychologizing of contact processes family members play psychological games, feed off one another, do "numbers" on one another, and generate friction out of sheer boredom. Abrasive patients bring these relational patterns into treatment. Psychotherapy becomes "the hair of the dog."

WAITING FOR GODOT

But why all the boredom? What are we waiting for? More than in any other period of history known to us, contemporary man distorts and toys with the concept of time. Opposed to Erikson's linear time and defined life stages, our experience of time and action is shaped by the tempo of our culture and the immersive stimuli of TV and other communications media. Through these we are drawn into temporal and visual proximity with distant cultures and events, bombarded by fictive imagery wherein past, present, and future merge; stupefied by dreamlike, incestuous machinations of the soap opera and incited to fantasies of murder, kinky sex, and action-packed dramatizations of violence and pursuit. Ordinary routine and mental life pale by contrast. Patients describe their lives as stale and flat, hectic and harassed, sometimes amusing but rarely joyous. Time drags or slyly slips away (Stern, 1977). The polarities of action and passivity are accented while the daily round of the middle range is endured as a sort of waiting game.

Based on his study of atomic-bomb survivors in Hiroshima and his later clinical work with American veterans of the Vietnam war, Lifton (1976) concludes that the theme of death and its relationship to larger contemporary experience, has so impeded the formative process— "man's essential mental function of symbol formation or symbolization"—as to foster a condition of psychic numbing, which by his definition, is "a form of desensitization . . . an incapacity to feel or to confront certain kinds of experience, due to the blocking or absence of inner forms of imagery that can connect with such experience" (p. 27).

Lifton calls attention to the extent in which we unwittingly characterize ourselves as survivors—"postmodern, postindustrial, posthistoric, post-identity, posteconomic, postmaterialist, posttechnocratic, and so forth," adding,

> In other writings I have emphasized the importance of holocaust in our symbolic vocabulary of the recent past (Nazi death camps, Hiroshima and Nagasaki, Vietnam), the present (beginnings of massive starvation in Africa and on the Indian subcontinent), and the future (imagery of ultimate destruction by nuclear weapons, environmental pollution, to other means). Now we see the imagery of holocaust coming together with the experience of modern cultural breakdown: our loss of faith not so much in this symbol or that but in the entire intricate web of images, rituals, institutions, and material objects that make up any culture. The urgency of contemporary innovation stems from this sense of survival and loss at the most profound experiential level. (p. 27)

These formations seem to provide at least a partial answer to the question, "Waiting for what?" Every American approaching the age of 37 has been faced with the implicit threat of sudden extinction. (In this connection I shall never forget the Christmas morning when I gave my 12-year-old grandson a tape recorder, anticipating his pleasure in building a library of his favorite music. He immediately taped an improvised speech on the threat of nuclear warfare, radioactive fallout, and total destruction.)

By the same token, every therapist over the age of 37 has had X-number of early years in which he and his primary objects have shared psychic representations that staked some claim to posterity. Thus, in addition to traditional generational differences there now exists this critical disparity of symbolic referents between the older therapist and the younger client. From this vantage point, the younger client may feel envious and even contemptuous of the older therapist for having shared in a more "innocent" world, while the therapist, even as he is abraded by the patient's narcissistic preoccupation, may feel justifiably relieved that his youth was not darkened by what I can only describe as cosmic grief.

Psychoanalysis has much to answer for its sanctioned detachment toward civilizational influences in interpersonal relationships. I have long been convinced, for example, that the revisualization of the marriages and demonization of husbands that took place in the six wives described was in large part an unconscious struggle to "cast out" their cosmic grief through projective personification of the impersonal nihilistic force they had internalized, onto their husbands. In this context, I have viewed the more hedonistic and destructive aspect of the Women's Liberation Movement as sanctioned diversions from the collaborative effort that must be initiated by men and women working creatively together to outlaw nuclear armaments, to enhance the quality of life through determined action, and to preserve the living future. It may appear that I have strayed far from the theme of the abrasive patient, but indeed, I am no longer able to confine my psychotherapeutic concerns to even the most advanced Freudian model. It seems utterly abrasive to me, today, to work within this circumscribed frame of reference.

REFERENCES

Eigen, M. (in press). On demonized aspects of the self. In M. C. Nelson & M. Eigen (Eds.), *Evil, self, and culture*. New York: Human Sciences Press.

Erikson, E. (1950). *Childhood and society*. New York: Norton.

Erikson, E. (1968). *Identity, youth, and culture*. Springfield, IL: Charles C Thomas.

Feuer, L. S. (1955). *Psychoanalysis and ethics*. Springfield, IL: Charles C Thomas.

Freedman, B. (1939). Psychosocial repression and social rationalization. *American Journal of Orthopsychiatry, 9*(1).

Johnson, F. A. (in press). The Western concept of self. In A. J. Marsella & G. DeVos (Eds.), *Culture and self*. San Francisco: University of California Press.

Langs, R., & Searles, H. F. (1980). *Intrapsychic and interpersonal dimensions of treatment*. New York: Jason Aronson.

Lifton, R. J. (1973). *Home from the war*. New York: Simon & Schuster.

Little, M. (1951). Counter-transference and the patient's response to it. *International Journal of Psychoanalysis, 32*, 32-40.

London, P. (1964). *The modes and morals of psychotherapy*. New York: Holt, Rinehart, & Winston.

Nelson, M. C. (1968). Role induction: A factor in psychoanalytic therapy. In M. C. Nelson et al. (Eds.), *Roles and paradigms in psychotherapy*. New York: Grune & Stratton.

Racker, H. (1957). The meaning and use of counter-transference. *Psychoanalytic Quarterly, 26*, 303-357.

Searles, H. (1965). *Collected papers on schizophrenia and related subjects*. New York: International Universities Press.

Spotnitz, H., & Meadow, P. (1976). *Treatment of the narcissistic neuroses*. New York: Manhattan Center for Advanced Psychoanalytic Studies.

Stern, E. M. (1977). Narcissism and the defiance of time. In M. C. Nelson (Ed.), *The narcissistic condition* (pp. 179-212). New York: Human Sciences Press.

Turkle, S. (1978). *Psychoanalytic polities: Freud's French Revolution*. New York: Basic Books.